# HOW CAN I UNDERSTAND MY KIDS?

# HOW CAN I UNDERSTAND MY KIDS?

Herbert Wagemaker, M.D.

WITH LEADER'S GUIDE BY DENNIS BECKER

Quotation from *Hide Or Seek* by James Dobson, Copyright © 1974. Fleming H. Revell Co., Old Tappan, N.J. Used by permission.

Quotation from *Conjoint Family Therapy* by Virginia Satir, Copyright © 1967. Science and Behavior Books, Inc., Palo Alto, Calif. Used by permission.

HOW CAN I UNDERSTAND MY KIDS?

Copyright © 1973 by The Zondervan Corporation
Grand Rapids, Michigan

This edition 1978

Leader's guide copyright © 1977 by Board of Evangelism and Christian Education of Mennonite Brethren Churches of the United States. Published by The Zondervan Corporation by permission of the Board of Evangelism and Christian Education.

All rights reserved. No portion of this book may be reproduced in any form without the written permission of the publisher.

**Library of Congress Cataloging in Publication Data**

Wagemaker, Herbert.
How can I understand my kids?
Published in 1973 under title: Why can't I understand my kids?
Bibliography: p.
1. Youth—United States. 2. Conflict of generations. I. Title.
HQ796.W2 1978 301.42'7 78-14955
ISBN 0-310-33942-1

*Printed in the United States of America*

To

Mary Ann,

Robyn,

Bobbi

and Lori,

good friends to share life with.

## ACKNOWLEDGMENTS

I owe Young Life, Inc. a great deal for allowing me to work with them these past ten years. Much of what I know about adolescents comes from this experience.

Men like Carl Rogers, Paul Tournier, Bruce Larson, Wally Howard and Keith Miller also have added to my understanding of human relationships. Their ideas are found throughout this book.

I also owe my parents, Mr. and Mrs. Herbert Wagemaker, Sr., a great deal. They taught me many things about life and God and made it seem worthwhile to get God and life together somehow. A very special uncle, Mr. C. B. Meyers, also did this for me.

My wife, and very best friend, Mary Ann, has been through much of this struggle with me. She puts up with me when my theory and my life don't match up. I'm grateful for Robyn, Bobbi and Lori who prevent me from being too theoretical and recognize that I, too, have feet of clay and have forgiven me many times for this.

Lynn Day typed and Arline Haufler corrected the manuscript. I can't thank them enough for this.

# CONTENTS

# Chapter 1

# What in the World Is Going On?

Bob Stark is nineteen. He's been at the University for two years now. He sits in my office in the Student Infirmary with his head in his hands, the picture of dejection. He came here with some great ideas, and soon became a spokesman for causes he considered worthwhile. He met others who were also for good causes—equality, freedom and justice. They banded together to work for these goals, yet two years later, this group has broken up because of internal friction. Feelings are hurt; people are angry. What were once love and understanding are now turmoil and disillusionment. Bob reflects these emotions as he talks to me.

"Everything seemed so perfect; we were all so involved in great things. I just don't understand how hate and bitterness can come out of something as beautiful as this."

Her eyes revealed her anguish. Jan Keys choked back the tears as I told her that the pregnancy test we ran on her was positive. She told me about the relationship in which she was involved. Jim had been a great guy when they first met. He was kind, considerate, thoughtful, everything she had hoped for in a guy. They started going together after Christmas. He had some "way out" ideas about living together, but they were in love, so she accepted his ideas and moved into an apartment with him. This was her first experience with sex. Then Jim had changed suddenly. No longer was he kind or considerate to Jan; he spent more and more time away from the apartment. They began to argue and fight until Jan was unable to take any more.

Not only was Jan breaking up with her boyfriend; she was facing a pregnancy that she certainly didn't want.

Ken and Bill were scared young men who wanted to see me together. Both junior psychology majors, they had read that LSD may cause genetic changes that could be passed on to their children. As they sat in my office, the two of them pieced together a story about their experiments with drugs. Initially, they had wanted to gain insight into themselves. They wanted to solve their problems, to find out more about themselves, to establish better relationships with other people. But one drug led to another. Their reasons for taking drugs changed. They became interested in the thrill, the high. Now they wanted to get off drugs and to find out if they had done *any* damage to themselves.

Bob's dad was a success. Bob described hi family situation for me. His dad dealt in real estate. He was also involved in politics and was part of the machine that ran his city. Every time Bob's dad bought property, a new road was put through it, or it was re-zoned for apartments or a shopping center. This happened too often to be mere coincidence, and right about the time Bob was figuring out his dad's schemes, Bob was caught cheating in high school.

"Dad was really uptight about this. I was grounded for a month, and my allowance was suspended for two months. About this time communication broke down between dad and me."

I listened carefully. Bob was describing the world we live in. Sure, we don't all get the chance to pull crooked deals the way Bob's dad did, but we all have our own little deals. For some of us, they involve income tax returns. For others, they might include getting a ticket fixed, or knowing the right people at the right time. This is the world that many of us let our children see. They know what's going on. They follow our leading. The big thing is not to get caught.

Jan's parents had been divorced since she was ten. Her mom worked. Jan was more or less on her own from an early age. She had an older brother, but he was away at school and she didn't see him very often. "I felt close to mom, but I didn't see much of her. She would come home from work tired . . . too tired to face the work needing to be done around the house. I felt lonely much of the time. When Jim came along, I thought he was great. For the first time in a long time, I wasn't lonely!"

Ken and Bill came from homes that on the surface, at least, seemed good. Bill's dad served on his church board. Ken's dad had been involved in civic affairs for a number of years.

Bob, Jan, Ken and Bill are real people. They have real problems. They are the products of our society. They are part of the new generation. What's so different about them?

Take Bob, for instance. He came to school full of idealism. He even implemented his idealism. He found people who felt as he did and became involved with them in trying to change things. After a year of trying, he found that these people had the same relationship problems that he had experienced, so he became disillusioned.

Jan Keys is another illustration of a broken relationship. Her story is more tragic than Bob's because her idealism led her into a relationship that was more vulnerable. She was led down a pathway that appeared wonderful, only to find that it wasn't exactly what it seemed to be. Good, productive relationships can turn into destructive ones over a period of time, almost without our knowing it. The change in Jan's and Jim's relationship took place when they decided to live together and she became pregnant.

Ken and Bill wanted insight into themselves. Their reasons for getting involved were good, but they chose a poor way of doing this. At least, it's questionable if any type of drug could do this for them.

What in the world is going on with kids, and why? Also, what can we do? Hopefully, answers to these two questions can be found within this book. The illustrations will be about *their* kids, not yours or mine. It would be nice if we cou[ld] stay impersonal, but sooner or later it will be *our* kids, yours and mine. What about that time? Will it be what we've dreamed about, or will it be a time of tragedy?

*Questions for Discussion:*

1. What in the world is going on?
   What are the things that make you "up-tight" with the new generation?
2. Is society responsible for this: Are parents? Is it just this generation?
3. What factors are playing a big part in what is happening?
4. What can be done to alter the situation?

# Chapter 2

# Credibility: Fact or Fiction?

Before we can really get into the questions of the last chapter on why young people are behaving the way they are and what we can do about the problems involved, let's listen to more of them.

John has gone to church all his life. Every time the door opens, his mom and dad are there. He's there, too, or he was. "I used to go all the time. I was even president of our young people's group. One Sunday a student from the university came to Sunday school. The elders and deacons had a quick meeting and the student was asked not to stay for church. He was black. We have a sign on the front of our church that says everyone is welcome. This isn't true, but the sign is still there. If the sign is a lie, maybe what the preacher says is a lie also. Maybe what I've heard in

Sunday school isn't true either. I'm really confused. The church says God loves, but *it* doesn't. I went to our minister about this, but he told me that the time just wasn't right yet. The church that told about God's love just wasn't ready to show love itself."

John wasn't alone in his confusion about the church. Mary's church had just completed a new Sunday school building. It cost more than $50,000 to construct. It had all the latest equipment. Someone in her congregation suggested that it be used as a nursery school for children of working mothers during the week, but church members reacted strongly. "What an uproar! Mothers were afraid germs would be spread around the rooms and that their children would be infected. These rooms are vacant except for two or three hours a week. Some working mothers lock their children up in their homes because they can't afford another place. I taught the kids in my Sunday school class this chorus on Sunday:

Jesus loves the little children
All the children of the world.
Red and yellow, black or white,
They are precious in His sight.
Jesus loves the little children
of the world.

For some reason this song has been going through my mind all week!" Mary hasn't dropped out of the church, but many of her friends have.

Joe broke the news to his folks that he was joining VISTA for a year. "What a response I got! You'd have thought that I'd joined the Foreign Legion for ten years or something. Dad hit the ceiling, and mom just sat and said nothing. Both of them were really disappointed in me. Dad said, 'These people wouldn't be in that shape if they would just work and help themselves. Why should you drop out of school and throw away a year of your life on people like that?'

"Yet Dad is Home Missions chairman, not only for our church, but also for the state in our denomination."

Jill and Frank came in to say "Good-by." Frank had just completed one year of residency in internal medicine and Jill was a laboratory technician. They had recently married and were on their way to India to set up a community clinic in a small village there. Scheduled to be gone for two years, they were excited and eager about going. The only drawback was their parents, and they had worked through this problem fairly well. "At first dad just couldn't see it. He sat down with me and told me how he had dreamed about the day I would graduate from medical school. When I did, he was overjoyed. His next dream was the office down the street from where I lived. He told me he was glad that now I could have the things he had always wanted for me, things that he couldn't buy for me. Why wasn't I content to practice medicine in our own community and make a decent living?"

What are these young people saying? One thing for sure, they suggest, there's a big difference in what we say and what we do. We talk about God's love, but we don't demonstrate it. We talk about helping people, but we don't go to them or encourage others to go. They're saying our lives don't back up our words. Quite an indictment. There's a real problem of credibility here.

May I be quick to add, they have a credibility gap of their own. What they say and proclaim is not always carried out in their lives, either. Just the same, some of what they're saying is true. Both young people and adults recognize the credibility gap. Now, what do we do about it?

*Questions for Discussion:*

1. Are adults credible? In what ways are they credible? In what ways are they not credible? Do they need to be?
3. Is the credibility argument (that young people use when talking about the church) a valid one?
4. What can we do personally, about the credibility gap?

# Chapter 3

## What's a Revolution?

"Four students were killed today at Kent State University. They died from. . . ." "Armored cars were used to quell a riot of students in Tokyo." "Police cars and the national guard moved into Watts." This type of revolution we hear about all the time. It's out where we can see it.

At other times, the crisis is even closer home—like my first experience, at age fourteen, as a driver in an auto accident. By the time my dad got there, our truck was pushed over to the side of the road. What a night. I had just received my driver's license, and had "gently" dented a car in front of me. The truck wouldn't function. In panic I rested against it. Not much need to talk; I couldn't have gotten a word in anyway. Dad never did listen well with his mouth open and that "look" in his eye. Here was born, at least to my knowledge, my revolution. I resolved to escape—get free—leave.

I remember the revolution, but the details are so vague, I can't put my fingers on them. At least, the illustration shows that we adults also had our revolution.

I had lunch with some friends the other day. Since we live in a college town, our thoughts drifted to college students. Someone said something about how kids are nowadays. Someone else said, "There's a small core of radicals, and they keep things stirred up all the time. If we could just get rid of them, we'd be okay, and we could go back to living . . ." (whatever that meant).

A study published by *Fortune* magazine states that there are twenty-three million Americans between the ages of 18 and 24. Eight million of these people are in college. Forty percent of these college students hold views, in general, that are in opposition to those held by their elders. The editors of *Fortune* went on to say that behind the small, radical minority of activists stands another minority. This group is large, comprising forty percent of our college and university population. They hold many of the same viewpoints as the activists, and their group is growing.

My revolution wasn't like that. I wanted to be independent, and so did most of my friends. Even so, our ideas were essentially those of our fathers. Yet something different is going on today. What is it?

Steven Kelman wrote in the *Saturday Evening Post* in 1966, that the revolution between the generations is taking a particular form—Skepticism. When I read this, the light went on. T[illegible] form of the revolution is skepticism. I wanted to be free, yet I never questioned my parents' way of life. Now, my way of life is being questioned. My friend at the table that day had said, "We're being asked why we live the way we do, and what's at the foundation of our existence. It would be bad enough if this were all they asked, but they're also asking me if my way of life is worthwhile. This really raises my anxiety level. The impudence of anyone who would ask this question of one who's lived twice as long. What do they know of life and its struggles?"

"Our way of life is being challenged," he continued. "I've lived life, worked hard, and become something. I'm ready to slow down—relax, look around some. I've 'made it.' Now some upstart tells me that this is for nothing? That my life has no meaning? He asks me if it's been worth it. Can't he see? I have a nice car, a house that's almost paid for, and children who are growing up. What's wrong with that?" He had fire in his eyes when he said this.

My father opened a bankrupt grocery store in the early thirties. I have vivid memories of playing in the big bread box with the various cats that were around. I remember sleeping on the burlap sugar sacks, and, at times, shooting my broomstick gun at an imaginary enemy as he crept up on my fort. More often than not, I was carried to the car, taken home and put to bed after the store closed. Mom helped dad in those days. They both worked hard; life centered around making the store go, and finally it became a successful business. They were determined I wouldn't have to work as hard as they did. They remembered how it was to be poor—what it meant to share roller skates with seven pairs of legs. I would have things, a college education, a chance at "life." This is what my parents invested their lives in—not really a bad investment, when you think it over. They knew what it meant to be poor. It wasn't a good feeling. They wanted to change all that. Now other changes are demanded.

Not only is our personal way of life being challenged; our institutional life styles are also being challenged.

A young man asks to speak to the elders of his church. "I'd like to know," he questions, "what you've been doing as a church for the last fifty years? Is the city different because you've been in existence?"

"Well, we've been right here, at least we've been here since we were forced to move out of the city."

"Yes, that's right. More of our people moved out of the neighborhood each year, and, finally, we moved out to the suburbs with them. We haven't become involved in many of the things that have been going on, we just live and let live. We do give baskets to poor people on Thanksgiving and Christmas though. We see our mission as getting people into the church, offering them Christ, and teaching them about Christianity."

"Tell me, what's happening to your young people?"

"Well, for some reason there aren't as many around as there used to be. Many of them have grown up, of course, and young people nowadays just don't seem to be interested in the chu[rch] the way they used to be."

We're in a revolution. It's all around us, not only in South America, Europe, Japan, Russia, but also in this country. My friend had said, "If only we could get the small core of radicals." Those words stuck in my mind all day. I even caught myself wishing the statement was true. But it isn't. A large number of youth are dissatisfied with material things, the church, the government; they obviously want radical changes in clothes, looks, music. They're pointing to something that's going on. Something's changing. This something is real, and the most disconcerting thing is, it's aimed at the very core of my existence. Everything that I'd thought was good, proper, and worthwhile they say is bad, improper, and not worthwhile. Now, I could brush off this attack without a second glance, if it were not for one basic thing. Down in the deepest part of me, I know there's some truth in what they're saying, and so I'm uncomfortable.

My American way of life has been good to me. I've gotten ahead. I've lived comfortably. But, the more I acquired and the more I advanced, the more I knew that there was an emptiness in me. I had to admit that the "good life" I enjoy was not enjoyed by everyone.

Sooner or later, the revolution will be on my doorstep, at my house. That's different from observing the revolution going on "out there." Suddenly, it's personal. It involves me. When it comes, how will I respond? What will happen? How will it affect me? How will it affect the people I love the most? And most important, what can I do about it? The subject of Chapter Four is the first phase in developing a solution. I can begin by listening.

*Questions for Discussion:*

1. When we talk about revolution, what do we mean? Have there ever been any good ones?
2. What about the "core of radicals" concept? Is that all there is to it? A concept?
3. In what ways is their revolution different? Or is it?
4. Will they grow out of it?
5. Are we, as adults, involved in any revolutions? Should we be?

# Chapter 4

# The Importance of Listening

There is hope for us "old folks." The revolution's going on, but there's hope that we can do something.

So far, each chapter has ended with a question as we've listened to voices to which we normally don't listen. It's good that we take time to listen to these voices, because they're saying something to us that is worthwhile. As a matter of fact, listening is one of the keys to the whole problem in which we're involved. Yet how often do we really listen to our children? Or do we, like Frank Nelson's father, "listen" by getting in our opinions first?

Frank is a college student, home for the Thanksgiving holiday. This is his first year in college. He's been exposed to many new ideas and experiences. He wants desperately to share them with his parents; so at the first opportunity he says, "Dad, I want to sit down and talk to you about school."

"Yes, I know all about school; I've read in the paper about all those radicals on campus and I've seen the pictures of all the guys with long hair and all the girls in their way-out clothes and I've heard what they've been saying and I've seen them.

"I'm real concerned about you, Frank, and about the influences that school is having on you. I also read in the paper that there are teachers up there who teach communism, and I'm afraid of the effect this will have on you. You're wearing your hair a little longer than usual, too, and I think it probably would be a good idea for you to get it cut. Now, what was that you wanted to talk to me about?"

"Nothing, really, I guess," Frank says as he walks out of the room. His dad has lost him through his lack of sensitivity and his inability to listen.

Simon and Garfunkle have some very good records out. One is entitled "Sounds of Silence." In this record, they sing about people who talk without speaking and who listen without hearing. Ask any college or high school student what this means, and he can tell you immediately. Let me try to interpret the song in a way that's meaningful. Let's start with the listening part. It refers to people who listen but don't hear. They feed into their own patterns of thinking words that other people tell them, so, instead of really *hearing* what they have to say, they *interpret* the words through their own thought systems. In other words, they screen out everything that's foreign to them or everything that doesn't fit into their own thought system. They hear words and they put them into their own thought patterns, but they don't listen because they have not grasped what the speaker wanted to say.

People talk without communicating, also. They do this by saying things that fit into the listener's pattern of thinking. In other words, they say things that they know he wants to hear rather than what's really on their minds. This is a rather devastating trap to fall into. We listen but we actually don't hear, and we talk but we *really* don't say anything. We don't reveal anything about ourselves nor do we find out anything about others. Our society has become so impersonal that all of us, especially the young, face this common problem. The result is a feeling of alienation.

Have you ever had the experience of talking to someone at a party and suddenly realizing that his attention wasn't focused on you? Maybe he was thinking about someone on the other side of the room or a business deal that he was involved in, but his attention wasn't with you at all. Perhaps right in the middle of a conversation, the person just left, or even in the middle of a sentence, he turned and went someplace else. I don't know how you feel when that happens to you, but experiences like this give me an uneasy, anxious kind of feeling. I feel uncomfortable, rather hostile and angry when this happens. I feel dehumanized.

On the other hand, when someone listens to me, I feel I have some self-worth in the eyes of that person. I feel that what I have to say or what I have to share is important to him, and that he recognizes my worth as a person. I get a sense of belonging. I feel that I have a personal relationship with someone which is more than superficial. I am received by another person as a somebody. Thus a good listener communicates non-verbally in a very special way.

Dave Wilkerson, in his book, *The Cross and the Switchblade,* states that the greatest problem of young people in the ghetto area is loneliness. Someone willing to listen can do much toward alleviating this problem. Listening and loneliness go together. By not listening to a person, we add to his loneliness.

This whole matter of listening is not a one-sided affair. Listening certainly helps the person who's being listened to, but in addition, it also helps the listener. When someone will talk to me, confide in me, and share himself with me, he tells me something about myself. He tells me I'm important as a person, that there is value in me. It's a tremendous thing to be trusted, and trust is given when a person confides in a friend. No one ever goes to another person and talks to him at more than just a superficial level unless he trusts him.

A person also receives a new point of view. What a great thing this is, to be exposed to something new—to look at something through the eyes of someone else, to be exposed to new concepts and ideas. Life is a continuous process of learning and the day we stop learning, we die. This does not necessarily mean that we die physically, but part of us does die. So, if life is to go on in an exciting way, we must listen.

The natural setting for listening is the family. Fortunately, parents are very special to their children. As a matter of fact, most children begin early in life trusting, confiding, bringing their problems and their concerns to their parents. Then, all of a sudden, they stop. The adoration and trusting attitude toward parents stops for a number of reasons, but one of the major ones is the parents' inability to listen.

We need to listen for our children's sakes, as well as for our own sakes. It's important that we don't lose contact with our children and that we don't lose contact with the world moving around us. The process of listening certainly benefits both the listener and the talker. Not only does it communicate verbally between two persons, but it also communicates non-verbally. Sometimes it even seems that what we communicate non-verbally is more important than what we say verbally. I need to listen. I need to listen to my own children. Through listening I gain a measure of understanding. When was the last time you really listened?

*Questions for Discussion:*

1. What is listening all about? Is it involved in communication?
2. What does it mean to you to be listened to? How did you feel when this happened to you?
3. How do we communicate to a person that we are not listening?
4. How did you feel when you knew you were not being listened to?
5. How can we help the people we talk to feel that they're being listened to?

# Chapter 5

# Sharing

Len Frank was seated in my office, telling me some of his problems. He told me how difficult it was to get into medical school; he mentioned his financial problems and his despair at ever working out his difficulties. His experiences rang a responsive note within me and made me listen intently. Then when he had finished talking, I couldn't help but share my experiences along these lines, in the hope of encouraging him, because I had gone through the same troubled times a few years before. My sharing was the natural outcome of listening. We listen and we remember similar life experiences. Thus a responsive note is struck within us. The next natural step in the sequence is the sharing of that life experience with the other person. Sharing, then, develops out of listening. It's important that we know a person, which results from listening. It is also important that we be known, a result of sharing.

I was walking down the street the other day and two boys were having a heated argument. They were standing toe to toe and eyeball to eyeball, and I thought any minute one would take a swing at the other one. As I came within hearing range one said to the other, "My dad can lick your dad," and the other one replied almost immediately, "My dad is smarter than yours."

This is the sort of image we all build up of our parents. We almost think they're super human, and in our opinion they can do no wrong. As a matter of fact, we put them on a pedestal. Now this is fine in some ways, but it certainly does break down the lines of communication between people. It's difficult to bring our problems to someone who we feel can do no wrong. Can you remember that remorseful day when you found out your father wasn't perfect? The day you found out he made mistakes, too?

This is a sad, disillusioning experience. At first we can't believe it, but then reality hits us. We experience many different emotions when we finally make this discovery. We are sad, resentful, angry and frustrated. When someone crashes down from a pedestal, he usually smashes on the cement floor below. Sometimes these pieces are hard to put back together again.

In a way, a parent enjoys being on a pedestal. It does great things for his ego. He's not really kidding himself. As parents, we know we're wrong and we know we're not supposed to be perfect, but at times our children don't realize this. Sharing helps them to realize it. We need to share with them the not-so-rosy parts of our lives, the parts of our lives that have been frustrating or rather unsuccessful. We have to descend from the pedestal anyway, and it's much better to climb down one foot at a time than to fall all the way down suddenly.) The end result is quite different, although in both instances we're down.

Len helped me to go back a few years. My college grades were average. They were a far cry from the standards set by medical schools for acceptance. I applied to over thirty medical schools. All the answers were the same. "Sorry." I told Len about coming back from Korea for one more crack at it. I remember going to Ann Arbor, where the University of Michigan is located, to try to take a course in physiology at the medical school that summer. The office was on the third floor. I walked up and down the stairs a half dozen times before entering the office. It took me an hour to muster the courage to ask if I could take a summer school course. Len was surprised. He had thought I breezed through everything. He didn't know how I had struggled. We had a great time of sharing, and he went out of the office with more insight into his problem, but with more than that. Both of us shared our lives with one another. We parted with a deeper understanding of each other.

Sharing requires us to be honest with our youngsters. In fact, we have to show them we really don't belong on the pedestal . . . that this is a figment of their imagination. Sooner or later they are going to come to this point by themselves anyway, but the process is easier for them if we gently open their eyes.

I remember how one night I went into the bedroom of one of my daughters after I had given her a spanking. I can't even remember why I spanked her, but I do remember going in there because I had to apologize, and it was a very hard thing to do. I had found out I was wrong in the situation and she was right. I had punished her without knowing what was really going on. The only thing left for me to do was to apologize for spanking her. I did this, with difficulty. Lori seemed to understand, though, and was forgiving in the whole matter. She was beginning to understand that I wasn't perfect.

John's dad was a prominent physician in a large southern town. Dr. Franklin couldn't wait for his son to finish college and get into medicine. He wanted his son to specialize in internal medicine and finally join him in his lucrative practice. There was only one problem with his plans. John was failing college. John said to me, "My dad has always expected me to be a doctor. I really have tried to live up to his ideal, and now my biggest fear is failing. Not only am I failing in school but I feel guilty about failing dad personally. My dad is a fine man and he has such great qualities. He works hard and he has dedicated himself to people and to his practice. I know this is going to be a tremendous disappointment to him." John had certainly failed; there was no doubt about it. He had managed to get C's and D's in all his classes—hardly qualifying grades for medical school. I'm hoping John and his father will be able to sit down and discuss their problem. It's important for John to realize we all fail, and for his father to share some of his failures with John.

This illustration shows how we need to share a part of ourselves with our children, a part we normally keep concealed: our failure. Once in high school I was cut from the basketball team. It was difficult for me to accept the fact that I had failed at something. I wished at the time for somebody to talk with about it. The adults I knew were strong people; at least, I felt they were. I didn't know they had failed, too. Now, as an adult, I realize I was living in an illusion. If I could have realized then that everyone fails, I would have been greatly encouraged.

What a great feeling it is to stop playing pretend. We can admit we're not perfect. Not only does the admission free us, but it frees the ones to whom we relate. They don't have to pretend either. They can share themselves with us, and thus contribute an element so important in a family relationship. This is the way it should be. God accepts us as we are. He accepts us even though He knows how we really are. Now, if God can accept us the way we really are, then we should be able to accept ourselves this way also. We're also free to accept others as they are. In this way we remove one of the large barriers that separates people.

Sharing does come out of listening; they go together. As a person, I need to know and to be known. This is not a simple thing. Sure, I am exposed in the process. But it would happen sooner or later anyway. Why not now?

*Questions for Discussion:*

1. What is involved in sharing? What are some of the good things? Are there any risks?
2. Do you think that most adults project an image of invincibility?

3. How do you deal with failure? Should we share it or hide it?
4. Should we demand that people share their lives with us? What if they don't?
5. What part does listening play in sharing?
6. Are there some things I shouldn't share with others?

# Chapter 6

## The Role of the Family

I spent much of my childhood on a street near a business district; that's where my dad's store was. Mom and dad worked long hours. Sometimes I woke up and heard dad leave the house in the morning. It was dark out. I knew it was early. Our family life centered around the store. I also remember that my dad was a man's man, strong and forceful. I admired him for this quality of manliness. My mother was a kind, hard-working, compassionate person. She involved herself in the lives of others. She had concern for poor people. She remembered how things were when she was a girl.

Then there was the smell of bread or cookies baking on a Saturday morning; there was a tramp through the woods on a sunny spring day and the discovery of thousands of blue violets covering the ground far back from the road. I remember running from one clump to another, picking them as fast as I could and handing them, full of excitement, to mom.

Family life holds memories for all of us. Growing up is a special time. Did you ever wonder what families are for? Why they exist?

The first time I saw my daughter, Robyn, many emotions welled up within me. I was proud and excited. I was filled with love for that little gal. I also realized how helpless she was, how dependent she was on us. It was great to watch her grow. She soon learned how to grab things and smile. Before we knew it, she was pulling herself up in the crib. I can remember her first steps. She was so proud of herself. Her face beamed with a big smile. When she fell, she stuck her arms in front of her, rose on her toes, and pushed herself up again. Walking gave her some independence. She needed help at first. It didn't take long, however, until she not only did not want help, she resented it. She wanted to be on her own. When she first started walking, I was rather anxious for her. I didn't want her to fall and hurt herself, but she did many times. She learned to walk in spite of all the falling. I'm glad she did. I wanted her to walk. What if she hadn't? I can't imagine how I would have felt about that, but walking by the crib of a deformed child gives me a small amount of insight.

One thing the family does is prepare a child to walk. If it didn't, the child would be a dependent creature all his life—a rather pathetic thing. Walking is one of the first ways the family helps the child become independent. There are many other ways the family prepares a child to be free and independent, prepares him to be a person who can leave the shelter and security of the home, venture into the world and function there as a responsible person. The family role, therefore, is one of liberation. This task lasts from the day that small helpless infant comes home from the hospital until the day he walks out the front door able to function on his own.

My daughters are growing up. I see it happening. They're bigger than they were last year. It's becoming more difficult for me to do their homework. I can't beat them at swimming anymore. I can't deny the fact that they're growing up.

I was sitting in a wedding of a friend's daughter the other day. Weddings bring out many emotions in me, but in this one I felt anxious. I was anxious, I think, because it brought to mind the fact that sooner than I wanted to, I would be giving my daughters to someone in a similar situation. I didn't want to. I'm not sure I do yet. I want them with me in the family. But I don't really. That wouldn't be good for them or me either. I must admit, though, that the anxiety I felt was real, and the wish to keep them dependent was strong.

It's painful to realize that the role of the family is to set our children free—to take them from dependence as a small child, to independence as a young adult.

I well remember Mike Graham. He grew up in the house down the street from me. His parents severely restricted him. As a young boy, Mike was held down. He could never come out and play because he had chores and other things to do all the time. When he grew older, he was still restricted in many ways. He couldn't stay out past 10:00 on Friday or Saturday nights. He was not allowed to get dirty while playing. He was the last one on the block to learn to drive. In high school, this process continued. Mike was not allowed to do the things other kids were allowed to do. During his last year, he became friendly with a rather tough gang of boys. They cut classes and in general stayed on the edge of trouble. One day they were caught with a stolen car. Mike ended up in jail. Emancipation was going on, but it was a struggle. Mike's parents didn't understand that the role of the family was to allow Mike ultimately to become free. They didn't realize that regardless of what they thought, he was going to be free. Unfortunately, his freedom was not gained in the gradual manner, and the explosion caused trouble.

Explosion is not the only way a person responds to a restrictive emancipation process in the family. Ron Brown is in his forties. He is a heavy drinker; as a matter of fact, he's an alcoholic. So far he's failed at everything he's tried. He has worked for large companies in management and once ran his own business. He's tried many things. He almost makes it, then he fails. He quits, gets fired, or goes bankrupt. Each time he fails, he goes back to the protection of his parents. They take care of him. He's angry, resentful, hostile. He detests being dependent, but that's how it is. His parents refused to let him go and tied him to themselves emotionally, so that now, he may never be free of them. They have destroyed his self-confidence to the point that his failures follow a predictable pattern.

You can see the devastating effect this type of

dependence has on a person's life. If I had helped my little girl up every time she fell, it would have taken her longer to learn to walk. She wouldn't have learned the value of struggle either.

So we encourage our children to take the first step. We're thrilled; they're happy. That first step starts in motion a process which lasts until the door closes and a person emerges who can function in the world independently. That person is my child. He or she has been involved in a process. The process started even earlier than his first step. It goes on even after he leaves home. The product of this process is a person, a very unique human being.

*Questions for Discussion:*

1. What are families for?
2. What is liberation? Is it a goal that you should set for your own children?
3. How do we go about liberating our children?
4. Did you have any personal struggles for independence as you grew up? How did you solve these problems?
5. What demands should we make of our children?

# Chapter 7

## The Key Relationship

My wife reminded me the other day that it had been fifteen years since I gave her an engagement ring. I had forgotten the date, but she hadn't. I was a graduate student at the time and drove down from Michigan to Georgia for the presentation. Everyone was excited about the big event. Her mother and sister wanted to know what was going on, what the ring looked like, had I given it to her yet, and so on. There was much talk in frantic, hushed tones. I was really playing it cool. There would be a right time and place for this event. It's a great experience to share this moment, this feeling with one you love. Few experiences add up to this one in life or even come close. Two people willing to share life, to be together, to start a family. What a great time. To love and be loved. Talk about a high, here it is and it's a natural one. Remember your great moment?

This was the relationship that counted. This was the one that made the family not only a possibility but a reality. Without it, there would be no family.

Time goes on. Children arrive. Responsibilities present themselves and we're busy attending to them. Sure, the relationship is still there. The family is together in most instances. But something has happened to the relationship over the years. Something is different. We've forgotten how it all started. We've forgotten some of what it means to share *love* with someone else. It's easy to forget amid dirty dishes, a messed-up house, and trouble at the office. Love still is, however, the key relationship in the family. Before the children came it was there. After they leave, it will be there. How about in between?

When we were first married, I was in graduate school. I couldn't wait to get home to share the things of the day with my wife. Some of this had to do with research, and there was no way she could be interested in it, yet when I reached home she was there waiting. We ate together and talked, and had a great time. She told me about her job, how her day went. Life was uncomplicated, rather simple for us then. I had been accepted in med school in the fall, and this was exciting. Our first baby was due in June, and that was also exciting. We went out a lot in those days. There were many friends in our same situation and we spent time with them. That year was a very happy one. We talked, shared, and loved each other. Yet two things were going to modify this relationship.

We moved to Philadelphia in the fall. I w starting medical school. Robyn had come to live with us, and she went along. Medical school was very demanding. I had to study. I'd come home at six, eat and lie down for thirty minutes. Then it was the books. I studied 'till twelve or one. At six a.m., the day started again. Saturday and Sunday were different, but I was always behind in school and worked hard to catch up. Robyn had demands of her own. Mary Ann was increasingly busy. I know she must have been lonely. Only two new factors had entered our lives, but what a difference they made. Now, it was a struggle to communicate. There just wasn't enough time. Robyn had to be cared for, a paper was due, there was an examination tomorrow. All these good things crowded in on our relationship. It became harder and harder to have a meaningful relationship. Sometimes it was impossible. At times, our arguments were very heated. Times have changed again. We have more children. Medicine is demanding. Other things also take time. Through all this process, I'm realizing more and more that our relationship is the key one in the family. It takes time to develop and time to maintain. I have to want to. I need to realize it's the key.

What happens if we as parents neglect our relationship? So much could happen. If I'm neglected or ignored, I become angry and hostile. If I become angry and hostile, I tend to pay back the person who made me this way. I can do this in many ways, but the best way is to confront the person with the issue. Get it out in the open. "I feel neglected, ignored, unloved. You're doing this to me." That's one way of handling our emotions. I wish we were all free enough within ourselves to handle things this way. I'm not.

Other ways of handling our emotions can be destructive. I can show my anger by not responding. I won't communicate. I won't show love. I won't support the other person. I'll build up doubts about her ability. This undermines her confidence and she can't function as well.

I can set my friends or our friends against my wife. Tell things about her. Do anything that will bring her down in their eyes.

I'll even work the children against her. I'll try to buy their love by over-indulgence. I'll set myself up as a protector of my children from her. I'll undermine her in every way possible. I'll also make the children dependent on me. I'll do everything for them, even though they can do it themselves.

We have all used some of these methods in the past in dealing with our husbands and wives. It's easy to see what destructive forces can operate through them. Can you see what a bind this creates for the child? Whom does he love? Whom does he side with? How does he handle the guilt which is created?

All of us are created to have warm relationships with others. The husband-wife relationship is the ideal place for this to happen.

Emancipation is the process in the family that sets the child free. A good relationship between husband and wife greatly aids this process. I don't like the anxiety I feel when I face the fact that my children are going to leave. Part of me wants them here with me. That doesn't alter the fact, however, that the process is going on, ar like it or not, it's happening to me.

They will be free. If the relationship between my wife and me has remained the key one in the family, the process of emancipation is a smoother one for all concerned. What relationship is the key one in your family? Are you sure?

*Questions for Discussion:*

1. What is the key relationship in your family?
2. How would you rate the relationship you have with your mate? Average, above average, below average?
3. Can you communicate how you really feel or think?
4. Do you feel free to be yourself in the family?
5. Do you spend time communicating with one another?

# Chapter 8

## Providing a Place

Ben Marshall wants a medical excuse to drop out of school. He needs some kind of reason to get out of his classes. He's flunking everything. His problem is deeper than this, though. I wish that just getting out of school could be the answer for him. Now twenty-one years of age, Ben has been at the university for three years. During that time he's tried three different majors, but all of them have proven unrewarding. He starts out with real enthusiasm, but after a while he loses his steam. He has also tried various activities on campus. Ben was in a fraternity for over a year, and was a member of a student activist group for a while. He's been into drugs. He goes from one thing to another to try and find something that satisfies him. He's looking for a place . . . someplace where he fits and where he can be himself.

Ben's case is not isolated. I see many young people in the same situation. It's important to share with you his family background. Ben's father is a highly successful businessman. His interests take him outside of the house or outside of the family on many occasions for long periods of time. As a matter of fact, Ben's father's interests are almost entirely outside the family. To compensate, his mother found interests in club work and social activities around the city. She's involved in many worthy projects and activities, but most of them are outside the family. Talking to Ben, I found that the happy memories he has from his childhood are all from experiences outside the family situation. His family was very impersonal; there was no real sharing, no warm relationships between any of the members. Ben is looking for warmth. Everywhere he goes he feels rejected, inferior, and unsure of himself. He never finds the security of the community that he is always looking for.

A community is a group of people who relate to each other. Each community is a very personal place; a place where people share their lives, their wants, their aspirations, their joys, their sorrows, their disappointments, and their frustrations. It is a place where they are loved and accepted as they are and where they feel comfortable. It is a place where they are allowed to grow and develop into what they are supposed to be.

Young people are teaching us a great deal about what community means. Many of them have formed their own communities where they can share themselves with others, get to know other people and be known by them.

Many of us have been taught that being self-made, strong, independent person is something very good. The rugged, self-made man is to be emulated. Our youngsters are finding out that to do this, we must hide much of ourselves behind a mask. We're just not this way, so we pretend. This point of view gets in the way of sharing one's life with another person.

Ben's father was like this. On the outside, he appeared to be a very strong person. He rarely showed any emotion. After coming back from World War Two, he started a small machine shop. He worked hard and built it up, until now he has many government contracts. He started with nothing, and now he has a big thing. He is a self-made man, yet in the process of becoming self-made, he neglected to take the time to live. He hid behind an impersonal mask and failed to relate to his family.

When young adults talk about community, they talk about a group of people. Sometimes these people share a house. They meet together and spend time with each other. It's really a place where people care for one another. They come, as they are, and they're accepted that way. It's amazing to me how young people so readily accept one another. Perhaps it's because each one realizes his own liabilities. A community is a place where they can relate with one another without masks. They're drawn together by common needs. So, this community becomes a place for them. This is what community means.

Paul Tournier, in his book, *A Place for You*, states that if a person finds a place or a community within his family, it will be easy for that person to find other places, throughout life, that provide community for him. If he doesn't find community in his own family, he will be like Ben Marshall, and will be constantly looking for a community, but having great difficulty finding one.

On the one hand, the task of the family is to help the child become independent, and on the other hand, the family is to provide a place, a community where he feels accepted, loved, and respected as a person. This seems like a paradox, yet the family needs to provide parts of both of these concepts for children. Children need to be free, but they also need to feel part of a community.

How does a family become a place? A community? Not without struggle and difficulty. It doesn't happen naturally, especially in the complicated life styles of today. Time, listening, sharing are some of the ingredients that go into the development of a community.

A community is started when people realize a need for one. It doesn't just happen. When do I start listening? When I realize the importance of listening. When do I share? When it dawns on me that my sharing frees others to do the same thing. When I realize that I need the help and support of others.

The community is developed on a going, give-and-take process. It's changing—it's moving. Throughout this process, children are given more and more responsibility and freedom. They're given more of a vote in family matters. They're allowed more and more freedom for discussion when the family meets to decide family policy. Providing a place helps the whole emancipation process by supporting a youngster in his first try at independent thinking or acting. It gives h the feeling of confidence as he shows some early signs of independence.

How do you define an on-going process? It's difficult. Because of my awareness of the concept of community and providing a place, I'm more aware when I do things to hinder that process. One night at dinner, my mind was on something else and my daughter told me she was moved up to a higher math group. I didn't hear. I wasn't listening. I went back and listened. She needed to be heard and recognized. Once again I was reminded of how I get in the way of this process. It's a struggle to get back on the right track. At times, I know I'm completely insensitive to the community process and thereby I hinder it.

Another way I hinder the on-going process of community is by pretending to be someone I'm not. As leader of the family, I'm inclined not to admit my own mistakes. When my wife reminds me of weakness, I'm short and defensive with her. I cut her off. If I could only lead (speak about—admit) from my own weakness and failure more often, this would free the others to talk about their failures and be supported through them. I could also get down from my pedestal to better footing. Our family would be a better place.

Another thing that hinders this process is my own uptightness. I can tell when something is getting to me when I feel my neck becoming tense and hard. Hair has become an important issue. A year or so back it was such a big issue that everyone in our group of adult friends was uptight about it. There was no way to talk or communicate about it. This was *why* we were uptight. There are many things today that make me uptight, and when I am, I affect the community which is my family. I stop them from talking about what they're involved in. I cut off communication. I can laugh about guys and long hair now, although it took me a while. It's taking me some time to work through some other things that I'm uptight about also. I'm changing, and I must continue changing if the family community is going to function properly.

What should a family be? A community, a place. Every member should be able to come and find love and respect, a place where he will be accepted as a person. The community is a place that offers support and understanding, even when things go wrong, and one makes mistakes or fails. It's a place where people can express themselves as people with rights of their own, and not be trampled down. It's a place where growth, development and change can go on, not only in the lives of children, but also in the lives of parents. It should be a great place. In this setting, we're all set free—to become what the great Creator of the universe has called us to be—unique persons, called for a unique task—to be a part of His great mission.

*Questions for Discussion:*

1. What kind of a "place" did you come from? How do you feel about your "place"?
2. Do we need "places"? What should they be like?
3. As parents, what kind of a "place" are we providing for our children?
4. What should our family communities be like?

# Chapter 9

## Providing Limits

Another important function of the family is to provide limits for the children. Here again, of course, is the problem of what kind, when, how do you enforce rules, and many other questions that can be complicated.

Frank was in jail. I went to see him. He came from a very permissive family. He could always do anything he wanted to; he could stay out late, he could have all the money he wanted, or have the car any time he wanted to. He told me his parents allowed him complete freedom. Because of their permissiveness, he felt they were unconcerned about him, that they didn't care what he got into. First, he started staying out late at night when he was in junior high school, then he became involved with a gang of boys who drank and caroused. They all became involved in petty thievery. They stole cars. He was in jail for breaking and entering. Frank wanted limits for his life. He tried to find them and he finally did. Unfortunately, they were the ones society imposes and not the ones his family should have imposed.

Tommie's situation was the opposite of Frank's. His parents were terribly strict. He couldn't do anything. He was made to study after school. He put all the money from his job in the bank. He spent every Sunday at church. His parents were vindictive with their punishment. They used physical means until Tommie grew older, then they took privileges away from him. He couldn't wait to get away from home to school. He now lives a completely undisciplined life. His limits were so rigid that now he lives without restrictions at all.

These, of course, are two examples of how not to discipline. But how then does one handle the problem of limits? What are limits supposed to do anyway?

Let's talk about permissiveness for a minute. Dr. Ginott in his book *Between Parents and Child* states that "permissiveness is the acceptance of children as persons who have constitutional rights to have all kinds of feelings." We must allow for feelings and thoughts. We all have them. At times they are rather bad. They can be nasty or destructive. They are a fact of life. However, if we act on these feelings, trouble results. We can have violent or destructive thoughts without repercussions but we can't act destructively without consequences. When I worked on the psychiatric ward of the hospital, we told patients there that they could think violently and they could express these thoughts verbally but they could not act on them. This meant that they couldn't be destructive or that they couldn't be harmful to property or to other people. Dr. Ginott also makes the point in his book that the right type of permissiveness brings confidence and an increasing capacity to express feelings and thoughts. No limits bring anxiety and increasing demands for privileges that cannot be granted.

Psychologists agree that limits of behavior must be established clearly. Dr. Fritz Redl uses this analogy. He divides behavior into three zones: a green zone, a yellow zone and a red zone. Acts that fall into the green zone are okay; they are sanctioned. A yellow zone act is a different thing. Behavior there is not sanctioned or approved of by parents, but it is tolerated. In other words, if a boy wants to wear long hair, this behavior is tolerated but not necessarily approved of by the parent. The red zone is still a different story. This behavior is neither approved, tolerated nor sanctioned. It includes things that endanger health or the welfare of the family or the family's physical or financial well-being. It also includes acts that are against the law. It is very important that these limits are set and that they are carried through. If acts take place which are in the red zone, for instance, punishment should be given out. Acts which take place in the green zone should be encouraged. The yellow zone acts are tolerated. Here we have a combination of permissiveness and also restrictiveness. Thus a child is aided in controlling his impulses and is given a chance to develop inner control.

Here again we must realize that the setting of limits or discipline is a learning experience. It can't be simply punitive. We must set limits because this shows children that we care for them and are concerned about them. But we must set them in such a way that they don't hinder or in some way alter the emancipation process. The specific limits for different families are going to be different. There are some types of behavior I can tolerate in my family which you can't tolerate in yours. There are also some types of behavior you can tolerate which I wouldn't be able to stand. The important thing is that limits be set with love and understanding, to help the youngster gain inner control.

When my daughters do something that's in the red zone, my first response is to get angry. "There's absolutely no reason for that. I will not tolerate that kind of behavior." And so it goes. At that time, I'm not ready to deal with anyone, least of all my daughter. My mind is completely closed. Okay, I recognize this. When the initial shock is over, I calm down. Now I'm ready to listen. Maybe there is a good explanation. I'll never know unless I listen. She feels that she's at least being heard, and I haven't reacted to the emotional charge of the moment. I've learned several things from talking to my girls at this time. They are fair and usually quite honest about the whole situation. I want them to come to me if they're in any kind of trouble. If they know I listen to and love them, perhaps they will be able to trust me if and when the time comes.

This is still another part of the process of community. Limits are an important part of any community. This fact is true not only for the family, but for all communities. Limits tell someone that he is worth enough not to be allowed to get into bad trouble.

Of course, as time moves on, more and more limits are removed, and more freedom is given. The goal is inner control, not outer. Many of life's situations fall into categories that aren't governed by rules and outer control. I don't need a rule book—I need inner control. I need to learn to regulate my behavior so that it is productive rather than destructive. If we can create this behavior in the lives of our children, they have reached an achievement which gives them a lifelong philosophy. This is one goal worth striving for.

Limits, then, tell a person something. The imposing of restrictions tells one we care enough about him not to allow him to do things which would be harmful to himself. The real goal, of course, is the development of inner control. The time will come, sooner than we expect, that external control will not be a factor. Young people are being exposed to all kinds of things. Drugs are a part of the junior high scene. Will your child have the inner control to resist things which are bad for him? Will he be able to say no? I hope so.

*Questions for Discussion:*

1. What good do limits do? What do they tell people?
2. What guidelines should we use in setting limits?
3. How should we enforce limits? To what extent should we go?
4. How can we make limits clear?

# Chapter 10

# The Birthright

"And it came to pass, that when Isaac was old, and his eyes were dim, so that he could not see, he called Esau his elder son, and said unto him . . . now therefore take, I pray thee, thy weapons, and go out to the field and take me venison, and bring it to me that I may eat. That my soul may bless thee before I die." Rebekah heard this conversation and went to Jacob to arrange for him to receive his father's blessing. She put goat skin on his hands and neck and cooked the food in the way Isaac liked it. The scheme worked. Instead of Esau, Jacob received the blessing, even though he secured it through fraud.

"I can't believe it. My brother has always been involved in all kinds of trouble. He smashed the car when he was in high school. He's flunking out of the university. He's been in trouble with the law but he still retains the position of the favorite in the family. He's selfish, unsatisfied, obnoxious, but he's still the one who gets the privileges. When I need money, I have to earn it. When he needs money, dad gives it to him."

The formal giving of the birthright or blessing isn't done much anymore. At one time, though, it meant a great deal. Bestowment of the blessing usually was reserved for the eldest son, and meant that he would take over the family when the father died. With it went the family riches and property along with the position of authority. It was a highly sought-after position. The family blessing was similarly coveted; it was not given to everyone in the family.

It seems that in most families, one child is picked out to receive the blessing or birthright. This child receives most of the favors and not much of the demands. The favored child knows he is "special," and the other children know it also. I've been told by many of my patients, "I was the favored child," or "My sister was the favored one."

Sometimes, this child is the real troublemaker. He can and does "get away with murder." Little is demanded of him. In many cases, he's the one who deserts the family in time of real need.

The amazing thing about giving the birthright is that in most cases, the parents don't even realize they have a favorite. The children know, however, and feel this injustice very acutely.

In reality, it's rather hard not to pick out a special child. The oldest child has a position of importance. Maybe he or she looks like you. That has to be important! Some children pick up more of our personalities and makeup than others. They have a natural "in."

The giving of the birthright has effects on all the children. If one is singled out, the others are left out. The demands and limits are different for them. They feel this, and at times, they are resentful.

Even if I'm not mindful of it, I give away the birthright. I tend to be harder on two of my children, and I naturally tend to pick out one for a special blessing.

Wouldn't it be great if we could give each child a birthright or blessing? Just think of what this would do for him, and how this would eliminate much of the competition and resentment among our children. The one way we *can* give each a blessing is by affirming each child as a special person, created by God in a unique way, for a special reason.

"My two years in India were the greatest experience of my life. I had a chance to live in a village there and work as an agricultural consultant. I helped the farmers there obtain a higher yield of crops from their land. The amazing thing about all this was the encouragements my folks gave me in doing this. They really affirmed me in my desire to drop out of school for two years and do this. I really shouldn't be so surprised about this! They've done this all my life."

This attitude on the part of parents is one of affirmation. Affirmation gives a person confidence and allows him the freedom to become the person he was meant to be. In my own life experiences, I've always done better in situations where

I was affirmed rather than in situations where I was torn down.

If our task in life is finding our own uniqueness and where we fit into God's plan, affirmation helps us to get some of the freedom which allows us to do that. Our affirmation, our giving a blessing or birthright, helps our children to be freed also. Each child needs freedom; each child is special in his own way. Each child deserves the birthright.

*Questions for Discussion:*

1. Who had the birthright in the family in which you grew up? What problems in relationships did this cause?
2. How did you feel about your position in regard to the birthright in your family?
3. Which child is the favored one in your immediate family? What does this do to the relationships in your family?
4. In what practical ways can you give each child the birthright?

## Chapter 11

# Looking at a Process

I must admit that my real or main interest in the problem of the generation gap is a personal one. That's not to say that I have no interest in what's going on around me in the youth culture—I have. Basically, though, for me, the generation gap occurs in my home with my own children. It's right where I live. I need to know, to relate, and to understand my own children. A tall order.

How I look at them is of utmost importance. I may try to push them down pathways I want for them. I may want to relive my life through them. I may want them near me, or dependent upon me. These feelings persist almost without my knowledge. Why do I want my youngsters to excel? For the good it does them or the ego trip it puts me on? Why do I push so hard in school? None of these questions can be answered either/or; there's always a cloudy area.

Let's try to look at a human being from God's point of view. Now, this discussion doesn't pretend to be profound, or the last word. Some of these ideas have been incorporated in earlier chapters, but it may be a good idea to look at them again. These concepts have helped me look at people in a different light.

What is the value of a human being? What are we worth? What are you worth? I appreciate human value when I go in to check my sleeping girls. Their value to me is overwhelming. Of course, personal value has to do with my relationship to the person. As we move out into the fringe of acquaintances and then into society, the value of individuals decreases. People are more impersonal here, and therefore, of less value to us individually.

What value does God put on human beings? I don't think anyone really comprehends how much He values us. We know that we are created in His image. Certainly, His invasion into human history as a person gave us a small glimpse of what He thinks of us. I know He considers us of great value, or He wouldn't have come. He wouldn't have died for us. This event should remind us of the value God puts on us. I can't help but think of this when I re-read the account of Christ's last week on earth as a man. What love and concern! What a price to pay for humanity! God places a high value on us, to say the least.

Have you ever noticed how people differ from one another? This is especially true or noticeable when we get to know people better. Each of us is unique. This was really brought home to me when our children started arriving. Were they different! They still are. How frustrating it is to learn to know one of them, and to expect the next one to be about the same. She's not. When the third one came along, I just gave up. They look somewhat alike, but that's where the comparison ends.

Scientists tell us we're different genetically. The things that go together to form personality, abilities, and other aspects of ourselves, are different for each person. We're unique, as far as biology goes. We share some characteristics as humans, but we are different in many aspects.

From God's point of view we're different also. Each of us has been given various gifts. The gifts are different. We have a uniqueness. If all of us were the same, then the body of Christians couldn't function. Paul makes this point clear when he compares the body of believers to the human body. We can't all be eyes. We can't all be arms. The body could not function if we were all the same. We're created uniquely from God's point of view.

We're also different because of our varying experiences in life. It's been known for a long time that everyone has a unique living experience. Even if you're brought up in the same family, your living experiences are different. There's a uniqueness in the way one individual relates to another. I can't possibly relate the same way to each one of my children.

We are unique genetically, socially and spiritually. Because of this uniqueness, we fit somewhere in God's plan for the universe. The big question is where.

Just where does my son or daughter, with his

or her own uniqueness, fit into God's plan? This question shifts the emphasis a little. It's no longer what I want for them, but what they were created for from God's point of view. The whole concept of discovery is here—the discovery of who they are and where they belong. We can help them discover where they fit, but we can't push them or direct them down paths of our choosing. I must be the one who ultimately discovers my place in God's plan. They must discover theirs. I must trust God for them. He loves them more than I do. I must also trust them.

What this basically means is that my children must be granted the freedom to choose. They must be allowed to become the persons they were created to be.

Tom and his new bride dropped into the office. They were on their way to Africa. Tom had accepted a job with a mission board to teach in a school for missionary children. This was a hard decision to make. Tom's parents were in their sixties. His father had suffered a heart attack six months before and was just recovering. Their decision meant leaving the United States for two years. "My dad fully supported me in this decision. I'll never forget the prayer we all shared around the kitchen table. Both dad and mom were thankful that we were following God's direction. They have really helped me discover where I belong, at least for the time being, as far as God is concerned."

What about failure? What if they (kids) choose wrong roads? An agonizing problem. If you've ever asked yourself, "Where have I failed?" you know what I mean. One of the realities of life is that at times, we fail. Real freedom allows the possibility of failure.

I wish all the stories were like Tom's. They're not. Recently I read the newspaper account of a young man who was killed in an automobile accident. I knew this young man well. He was experimenting with drugs and died with the evidence that he was using them at the time of his death. A tragic story.

At times it's hard to let our children have the freedom to go down right pathways. How hard it must be to see them take paths we know are wrong, pathways that can only lead to destruction. Hopefully, through the whole process of emancipation, their inner controls are being developed. Hopefully, their behavior will be constructive rather than destructive. I must admit I've asked the question, "Why?" on more than one occasion.

Can we really allow freedom? Freedom to fail? Freedom to become what God wants our children to become? Freedom to choose? My willingness could depend on my own degree of freedom. It also means that I have to be open to different points of view, my children's and God's.

So the task is one of discovery: the discovery of what my children were created for and where they fit in God's unique plan. This is not a simple task, or one that is answered once and for all. It's a task that continues for as long as life in the human form goes on. Not only does it go on for a period of time, but the place my children fit into now may change with time. It's an ongoing, changing process.

I've asked myself, "How do you really look at your three girls? Are they pawns that you simply move on your board of life? Are you really trying to help them discover where they fit? What if God's plan for them conflicts with yours? What if they make bad mistakes?

I don't know the answers to these questions. I know I must ask them of myself and not hurry over my answers. Somehow, I must help my girls in this process of discovery. It's imperative that they discover who they are as individuals and where they fit, with all their uniqueness and gifts, into God's great universal plan.

*Questions for Discussion:*

1. Are we, as human beings, really unique? In what ways?
2. What does your own uniqueness mean to you?
3. What part should "discovery" play in raising children? How do we help a person "discover"?
4. What does process mean to you? How does this concept fit into our lives?
5. Are you comfortable with the changes "the concept of process" has woven in it? Why? Why not?

# Chapter 12

# They Are OK

Thomas Harris, in a very interesting book, *I'm OK, You're OK,* goes into the practical aspects of relating. He states that each person has three basic parts: a parent, a child, and an adult. I know I have a child part of me because I act like one. I pout, become sullen, withdraw, feel hurt and do many of the things a little boy does. I also see myself as a scared little boy from time to time. My parent part comes out when I lay down the law; this is the way it is, the way it has been and the way it always will be. Period, Amen. I got my "parent" from my early experiences with do's and don't's that were handed down to me from my parents and other adults. These rules I accepted without question at that time, because I was too little to do anything else. I, in turn, do the same things.

I recognize the "parent" in my girls also. They

dictate, too. Robyn tells Bobby who tells Lori, who tells the cat what to do.

Along with the early development of the parent and child parts, the adult is developing also. The adult part resembles a data processing computer. It computes the information it receives and comes to a decision through this process. It looks at the data in the parent to see if it is true or false, to determine if it is usable for today, and then decides to accept it or reject it. It also examines the feelings of the child to see if they are appropriate at the present time or not.

The adult takes in the information, "stoves are hot," and looks at it. Is this really true, or can I disregard this information? It doesn't accept the parent dictum that "stoves are hot" on face value.

Along with this concept, that each of us has within him a parent, child, and adult, comes the idea that there are four life positions. Very early in life, a child picks up the idea that "I'm not OK." He also realizes his parents are OK. The first position then is "I'm not OK, You're OK."

During the first year the child is held, loved, cared for. He derives pleasure from this. He looks at his mother and says, "You're OK." After the first year, this attention decreases. Now he looks at his mother and says, "You're not OK" after all. This position is "I'm not OK, you're not OK."

The next position is "I'm OK." "You're not OK." This position develops out of an abnormal situation when the child is brutalized, and left to heal. He says, "I'm OK if you leave me alone by myself." This happens more frequently than we would like to believe. Five times an hour in our country, small children are battered by their parents. If this continues, aggression will be carried out against the "not OK" person-society-thing that's out there. These people end up in prison many times.

The fourth position is "I'm OK, You're OK." The first three positions were incorporated early in life. "I'm OK, you're OK" came first, and for most people, persists for life. For some unfortunate children, position one is exchanged for positions two or three. One of these positions is fixed into a personality at three years of age. To move into the fourth position takes thought, reason, action, and most of all, experiences that tell a person he's OK.

The goal of transactional analysis is to enable a person to have freedom of choice and the freedom to change . . . the ability to become "less uptight." The freedom to become "I'm OK."

Do I relate to my children with my own child-self? Do I withdraw, or pout, or get overemotional? Do I relate mostly as a parent by laying down the law or having a closed mind about many things? Or am I relating most of the time as an adult who gathers data, processes it, and arrives at a conclusion? We don't really relate if we act like our inner parents or children; we respond or react. Children react or respond with their inner child or parent part of themselves, also. When they do and I do, there is no communication. Only when we both act through our adult state do we communicate. This is what listening and sharing are all about.

For me to act as an adult, I must get the idea that I'm OK. Being "not OK" makes me defensive and uptight. When I'm like this, I react with my child or my parent, not my adult, and I don't really communicate.

What makes me feel I'm OK? How can I change from being not OK to becoming OK? In Christ, I'm a new person. Once I was not OK, but now, I'm becoming OK, and one day, I will be completely OK. Sometimes I feel that I'm really becoming OK. Other times, I'm discouraged, and feel like a helpless little boy who is insecure, fearful, and who does everything wrong. At these times, I find strength in reading Romans 8 where Paul talks about belonging to God's family. Even when I feel "I'm not OK," God accepts me as being OK. He's adopted me into His family. My Christian community also re-affirms my OK-ness by accepting me, no matter what.

"One Up" is a game. It's played by many people, including parents. Two people play at a time. No matter what happens in the game, one person always is up or above or better; the other person is always down or below, or worse. The people who play stay in the same positions until one decides not to play anymore.

"Bobby, do your homework." "But dad, I've got to get to the store before it closes so I can get some material for my dress." "Bobby, do your homework." There was no communication there, just ultimatum. One up, one down.

"Why did you get a C in math?" "Well, it was just too hard, I . . ." "I can't believe you got a C." "You don't understand." "Oh yes I do, no more T.V. or nights out until you get that grade up!" And so it goes.

Sometimes we get our children in a bind that gives them two choices, both of which get them in trouble. The person who is in the down position, remains there.

What happens when this type of game is played? Just think for a minute how you felt when you were the one down. I felt angry, frustrated, mad. I wanted to fight, to get even. That's what went on emotionally. I got even, all right. It may have taken some time, but I evened the score. One thing is for sure, there was no communication.

A similar game to One Up is "Put Down." "Kids are all alike nowadays, they're shiftless, lazy, have no respect for authority . . . etc." No matter what is said or done, the person is put down. The emotions that go along with "put down" are the same as the ones that go along with "one up." I get mad when people do this to me. It ends our communication. I don't want to communicate.

I remember I was really hurting one time. In desperation, I went to a friend to tell him what was on my mind. I wanted to share something that really bothered me. He laughed, told me he was surprised I had such a problem and gave me some glib, simple answer. I felt I was really put down. I didn't go back to him again when I had a problem. I couldn't stand that type of treatment. I couldn't stand being put down. There was a time in my life when I didn't even know I was playing these games, and simply went right on. The "parent" part of me governed my relationships with my kids and even others with whom I came in contact. Now, I realize I do this, and make an attempt at not doing it.

My discovery came one day after dealing with emotionally disturbed people. The doctor and the patient are usually in this one-up, one-down situation. For a long time, I didn't understand what was going on. There was no communication, and my patients didn't seem to make much progress. Then it dawned on me. The patients are always sick, while I'm always well; they always lose, I always win; they're wrong, I'm right. As we started to relate as equals, they responded; they were able to talk, to reveal what was going on with them. I also shared my life—good and bad —with them. Something happened to our relationship. We communicated. They were free to show themselves.

How does a person feel when he's one down, or someone else is one up? We've already gone through the emotional part of it, the anger, frustration, hate, but he also feels he's not OK. If I look at myself as being not OK, I can't function. If I'm told that again and again, this puts a stamp on me and I feel inferior, fearful, no good, worthless. Everything I try is doomed to failure. Nothing works.

The people who play this type of game usually don't feel OK themselves, and, in an attempt to feel OK, they put down others.

It's natural for parents to play one up or put one down. We all do. When kids are young, it's the way we relate to them. "Don't cross the street, don't play in the fire, eat your food, go to bed," are ways we communicate. Kids learn fast, however, that this means they can't handle things themselves. They're not OK; they're wrong. If we want to help them out of that situation, we must communicate to them more through our "adult" as they grow older. This tells them they are OK.

If my girls are to grow and develop into independent young ladies, they must realize they're OK. I must let them in on that bit of information by telling them, "You're OK." I do this best when I'm OK myself.

One of the greatest things we can do to another person is to say, "You're OK. You're worth something." This kind of experience happened to me the other day. My research grant had been turned down and I was feeling low about it. I was feeling worse than low; I was angry. I was told in so many words that I wasn't OK to do this type of work. Then the head of my department talked to me about it and said, "Our department will back you in this research. We think you can do it." He really told me, "We think you're OK." I can't tell you how good I felt then. I felt affirmed as a person. My attitude, my disposition, even the way I walked, were affected. I was on top of the world, for a while at least.

My children need this affirmation also. They need to be told they're OK, just as I do. I must relate to them more as equals, and less in the up-down position.

If I think I'm OK in your eyes, I'll have a tendency to let you know what's going on inside with me. I'll dare to do it. If I think you think I'm not OK, I just won't take the chance. My children act the same way. They won't risk a put down.

*Questions for Discussion:*

1. Do you recognize the *parent*, *child* and *adult* in you?

2. In what ways do you relate through these different selves?
3. What games go on in your family? Are people in "up-down" relationships with each other?
4. Do your kids know they're OK? How can you tell them?
5. Are you OK? What do you need to feel OK? Who can help you feel this way?

# Chapter 13

# The Solution, a Starting Point

It's personal, it starts at home, my home. It's me. This is where the solution starts. It's not them, or those, or she, or he, it's me. "Me? How can that be?" "It's me all right." "No, no way." "Yes, it is. It is me. If it's going to be different, if there's going to be a change, it starts here, with me."

I wish I could say that the task is easy. After all, I am forty and changing *me* isn't all that simple. There's been a long life of habits and attitudes which have made me the way I am. Besides that, I don't want to change. They—they're the ones that should—they're young. Why, for them it would be simple.

Where does change start anyway? With me, the starting point is attitude. It comes in looking at something a different way. It's the development of an openness to various alternatives.

We're taught at an early age that the basic presuppositions of Christianity are true and therefore they don't change. What I failed to see is that my Christian life is a process, something which is constantly changing. I discover new things in God's world. I'm exposed to new ways of looking at things through the Christian community of which I'm a part. My Christian experience modifies and changes my whole life. My Christian belief hasn't changed; I've just discovered some new things that have been around for a long time. I get uptight when I think change is destroying the very structure of beliefs on which my life is based. When this happens, I have to stop and ask myself if this is really true. Is this new thing eroding my Christian foundation? For instance, does long hair erode my foundations? Or is the problem just my uptightness? If it is merely my uptightness, how do I deal with my emotions? It's difficult to separate those issues that threaten our belief structures and those that don't. We could go into many of them.

One way that helps me deal with my uptightness is to discuss it in a group of Christians. Often they can shed new light on the subject. I find that some of the things I thought were very important issues really were not. I was letting myself become emotionally upset over nothing, or at least, over an insignificant matter.

Does being uptight affect my relationship with my daughters? I must admit that it does. At these times I turn them off and they tune me out. There is no communication.

If my uptightness affects me this way, how do I deal with it? Can this be changed at all, or am I doomed to a life of uptightness? I hope

I can change; I don't want to live my life uptight most of the time.

The opposite of being uptight is being free. How do I become free? I needed to start in the attitude department first. I learned this the hard way. I saw many students who were involved with drugs when I worked at the university infirmary. I gave many lectures and talks to them about the harmful effects of drugs from my point of view. They didn't come back. Then it dawned on me that perhaps they had a right to their own point of view, even though it was destructive. This freed me to listen and be open to them.

I was uptight about sex also. More lectures and advice were forthcoming. Again, the light was turned on, and I could at least listen to another point of view. The surprising thing is that I don't think I've changed my basic standards on these subjects at all. I did, however, become freer in allowing others their point of view. Then they began coming back to me for help when they were in trouble. These experiences freed me, made me less uptight, but I spent over three years just getting started.

I said my basic beliefs haven't changed about drugs or sex. What did change was the way I was looking at people who were doing things I didn't condone. I was able to relate to them. The up-down position was gone. We were more equal, and I was less uptight.

During this time I was also forced to reexamine my own standards for living. I was using my adult nature to determine if they were true, false, and relevant. I threw out a lot of rules that I thought were important at one time in my life and I felt as if I were dropping a sack of garbage off my back. I felt two hundred pounds lighter. I had to clean out a lot of trash to become free. God gave me the freedom to do this.

I also learned that I tried to control people by inflicting upon them my value system. That keeps me good, them bad; me up, them down. When they resisted this type of control, I became uptight. I learned that a person has a basic value apart from his value system and belief structure, even though it differed from mine. I really had trouble with this one, and still do. It's hard for me to view a person as a person, apart from his behavior and morals. However, the more I'm able to do this, the less his way of life makes me uptight.

As a Christian, I've been told most of my life what a miserable sinner I am. For some reason, this fact has stuck with me. It was a real struggle for me to see the other side of that coin, that God loves me and accepts me as I am because of Christ. That first bit of information kept saying to me, "I'm not OK." For a long time, I operated out of the "I'm not OK" bag, with rather devastating effects on my relationships. I had to prove to me and everyone else that I was OK. If I lost in a game, or someone saw things from a different point of view, I was put down and remained uptight most of the time.

For some reason it took a long time for me to realize that God loves me and it's all right for me to love myself. It's all right for me to see that I have value as a person. This means to me that I don't have to prove it. I don't have to control, I don't have to be right all the time. Now people can disagree with me and it doesn't crush me. I can look at another point of view without feeling that it's a personal attack on me. I'm freer now, because I'm OK.

With this new freedom came the ability to allow other people to be free. I didn't have to control them. I simply wasn't that uptight anymore. I could enjoy others for what they are: special acts of God's creation.

All this has helped me relate to my own children. I'm beginning to see them in a new light. They're unique; they're not like me. They may have different points of view, they may act differently. They may even go in different directions than I do. I must allow them the freedom to choose. I need to show them direction, but I do that through my own life as they see my source for meaning in life. If God is an important person in my life, they will see that. I need to help them become independent to discover their own uniqueness. They need to hear, "You're OK," so they will have the courage to explore, to discover. I can't play "put down" with them. I need somehow to communicate to them that life is great, that it can be rewarding and very worthwhile.

I've come to look at my task as a parent as not one of pushing, shoving or making into, but one of helping in discovery. I want my daughters to discover what life is all about for them. If I'm ever going to be able to come close to this goal, the lines of communication between us must remain open. They have to know that no matter what, I think they're OK, and they have great value to me, not to manipulate or make into, or shove, but as real, live human beings. This is the only way to bridge the generation gap.

*Questions for Discussion:*

1. How can I become freer as a parent? What gorbage do I need to get rid of?
2. What kind of a bag do I operate out of? An OK one? A not OK one? What effect does this have on my children?
3. What is my task as a parent? What helps me in this task?
4. Do the principles that we've talked about help us in other relationships besides those of our children?

# LEADER'S GUIDE

# Introduction

"Bridging the Generation Gap" is what *How Can I Understand My Kids?* is all about. How do young people think? Why do they think as they do? What can I do to understand them? What can I do to help them to understand me? All of these are important questions in raising teen-agers. The aim of these sessions is to help parents answer these questions and to help them build bridges to their teen-age children.

Several chapters in this guide were written by members of the Family Life Education class at the Mennonite Brethren Biblical Seminary in the winter of 1977. Special thanks are due to Dr. George Konrad, instructor, and Lowell Adrian, Dewayne Isaac, Robert Brazie, Al Gilbertson, and Bill Shamp, students who contributed chapters to this guide.

At the end of the guide is a list of suggested books for further reading. Be encouraged to look into these, especially *You Can Have A Family Where Everybody Wins* and *I'm OK, You're OK.*

This leader's guide suggests a great deal of student discussion, some small-group discussion, and other types of interaction. You are encouraged to use these as much as possible to help the students discover answers to their problems for themselves.

There are Scripture references to be used with each lesson. Always remember that the text, while not using Scripture references as a base, is not intended to replace the study of Scripture. Be sure to use the Bible study sections of each lesson. This will provide a base for continuing discussion.

Session 1

# What in the World Is Going On?

*Text:* Chapter 1

*Set Goals for the Session:*

1. Students will study some of the feelings and values of young people.
2. Students will compare the values of the examples in the text with the values of Scripture.
3. Students will relate to young people in a loving way.

*Prepare for the Session:*

1. Read the entire text before beginning the series of lessons.
2. Reread chapter 1.
3. Study carefully the Scripture references in this leader's guide.
4. Notice the different kinds of learning activities. Use as many of these as you have time for and

your class feels comfortable with. Be sure to include the Bible study section.

5. If you have a guest lecturer, invite him early enough to allow him time for preparation.
6. Prepare assignment sheets for the group discussion. Type the name of the example and the two questions given on each sheet.
7. Prepare your lesson outline,

*Scripture References:*

Ephesians 5:17-21; 6:1-4
Deuteronomy 6:4-9
1 Samuel 3:11-14
Ephesians 4:1-3, 25-32
Philippians 1:6

*Presentation:*

**FOCUS**

1. What is the "generation gap"? Is there really a "generation gap" or a "communication gap"? Why do you feel this way? Is a "generation gap" really necessary?
2. What can be done to close the "generation gap"?
   a. From the point of view of older people?
   b. From the point of view of young people?

**DISCOVER**

1. Group discussion
   Divide the class into four groups. Have each group take an example from the beginning of the chapter (such as pages 9-11) and talk about the following questions:
   a. Why do you think these young people became involved in the activities mentioned?
   b. What might their parents have done to avoid this kind of involvement?

   After allowing adequate time for discussion,

have the groups report their conclusions. Allow more time for class discussion according to interest.

2. Guest lecturer (optional)
   If a career youth worker is available (counselor, high school principal, youth director of a church or organization), you might ask him to present a lecture on what is happening in the youth scene today. Be sure to leave time for questions and comments.
3. Questions for discussion
   Talk about the questions for discussion at the close of the chapter in the text. Be sure to answer these in relationship to what is happening in your lives, not just what is happening to other people "out there."
4. Bible study
   The basic problem in all of the examples given seems to be a lack of good relationships with other significant people. What can parents do to develop good relationships with their children? Study the following Scriptures for principles and then build your own applications around the principles.

   Ephesians 5:17-21; 6:1-4
   Deuteronomy 6:4-9
   1 Samuel 3:11-14
   Ephesians 4:1-3, 25-32
   Philippians 1:6

After you have the class study these Scriptures, either individually or in small groups, allow time for discussion and the listing of principles and applications in separate columns on the chalkboard or overhead projector. Some of the principles which you will find are—

—Parents and children can both be subject to one another in the "fear of Christ." Parents may not have all the answers.
—Parents should not only teach their children verbally but should also be a godly example for them. This builds credibility into what they say.
—Parents should rebuke their children when they do wrong. They should not let them go unchecked in their conduct but at the same time, they should foster independence in the children.
—Parents should not act as rulers over their children but they should live in humility, gentleness, patience, and love. Parents and children should speak truthfully with each other and be quick to forgive.
—Parents should entrust their children to God, knowing that He can finish His work in them.

In this discussion, be sure to move from principles to concrete applications. What can you do to put these principles into practice with your children?

**RESPOND**

1. Think of one young person—either your own child or someone else with whom you need to develop a better relationship. What will you do this week to give a "listening ear" to find out what that person is feeling or thinking?
2. Close with a prayer of thanksgiving to God for building a relationship with you, of confession where you haven't built relationships, or commitment to building a relationship with one person this week.

*Assignment:*

1. Take time to build a relationship with one person this week. You will have opportunity to share your experiences next week.
2. Read chapters 1 and 2 in the text. Think about the questions at the end of chapter 2.

Session 2

# Credibility: Fact or Fiction?

*Text:* Chapter 2

*Set Goals for the Session:*

1. Learners will understand the importance of credibility.
2. Learners will understand how credibility is established.
3. Learners will examine their own lives and check their credibility.

*Prepare for the Session:*

1. Read chapter 2 of the text.
2. Study carefully the Scripture references given in this leader's guide.
3. Use as many learning activities as possible with the group.
4. Prepare your lesson outline listing learning activities, questions, lecture you will use.

5. Conduct a mini-survey asking several young people the following questions:
   a. Are adults credible?
   b. In what ways are they credible?
   c. In what ways are they not credible?

*Scripture References:*

James 2:14-18, 3:13-18
1 John 3:7-8, 16-18

*Presentation:*

**FOCUS**

1. Give the group an opportunity to share their experiences of relating to young people during the past week. How did young people respond when someone took the time to listen to them?
2. Think of a time when someone did not follow through on a promise they made to you? Or a time when someone's actions did not agree with what they said?
   —How did you feel about that person?
   —Did the incident affect any future relationships?

   Share your feelings with the group.
3. Report on your mini-survey with youth.

**DISCOVER**

1. Define "credible." (Capable of being credited; worthy of belief, entitled to confidence, trustworthy, reliable)
2. What do the following Scriptures say about credibility?

   James 2:14-18; 3:13-18
   1 John 3:7-8, 16-18

   —It is the practice of righteousness, not saying we are righteous, that makes a person righteous.

—People know what is real in our lives by how we live. Our lives indicate what our real attitude is.

—Our true faith and attitudes work themselves out in daily living. If our faith does not show, it is not real.

—If we have the presence of God within us, it shows in our daily conduct.

3. Review the examples in the text, pages 15-17, and answer the following questions about each example:
   a. What are the adults saying with their mouths?
   b. What were they saying with their actions?
   c. What were the young people hearing?
   d. What was the effect on the young people?
4. Again reviewing the examples in the text, what would you do if you were the adults involved in each example? Why? What do you think Jesus would do? Why?
5. Discuss the questions for discussion on page 18.

**RESPOND**

1. Each person should ask himself, "In what areas of my life do I need to be more honest so that my words and actions agree?
2. Close with a prayer of commitment telling God what you will do about your needs and asking for His help and presence.

*Assignment:*

1. Check your actions during the week to see if they agree with what you believe and what the Scripture teaches.
2. Read chapter 3 in the text. Think about the questions at the end of the chapter.

Session 3

# What's A Revolution?

*Text:* Chapter 3

*Set Goals for the Session:*

1. Students will learn what a revolution is and the premise for a Christian's revolution.
2. Students will begin to determine if Christians are to be involved in revolution.

*Prepare for the Session:*

1. Study carefully chapter 3 in the text.
2. Study the Scripture reference given in this leader's guide.
3. Prepare your lesson outline. Make careful preparation for any verbal input you will give.

*Scripture Reference:*

Luke 14:1-35

*Presentation:*

**FOCUS**

Definitions:

Author's definition: In general, a revolution is a view that is in opposition to those held by others. An example of a revolutionary attitude is being skeptical of the way of life of the elders.

General definition: Revolution is a fundamental change, a renunciation of one method of rule and the substitution of another.

1. Why does the word *revolution* always carry a negative connotation? Did we as a nation become free, to our knowledge, through revolution? Does "revolution" mean going from something good to bad, or going from something bad to good? What determines the direction?
2. List some characteristics of a "revolutionary." Define a "radical." (He advocates radical and sweeping changes in laws and governments which he believes will equalize social conditions or remedy evils.)

**DISCOVER**

Study Luke 14:1-35

1. In verses 1-6, what did Jesus do that was against the laws of that day? Do you control the law or does the law control you? Are we made for the law or is the law made for us? Jesus superseded circumstances (laws) for more important matters. He did not allow laws to control Him; He controlled laws.
2. Jesus upsets the tradition in verses 1-6, but in verses 7-11 He gives us one basis for being able to control the laws. What is one of the truths in these verses? (Humility; the key to being first is

being last.) What does this mean in regard to our present-day life style and philosophy? Are we willing to be No. 2?

3. In verses 12-14, Jesus talks about generosity and charity, the reasons for our giving. What is our attitude toward giving? Our attitude should be that of giving willingly because of whom we are giving to.
4. When confronted with personal change of plans, ideas, or of life situations, how do we react? How did the three men react to a call to a heavenly banquet in verses 15-24? (They gave three excuses: a. business, b. possessions, c. personal pleasures.) Do we ever use the same excuses?
5. In verses 25-33, Jesus talks about counting the cost. No man need become a student unless he is willing to count the cost of learning. What does Jesus mean when he talks about "subordination of self" in counting the cost? In today's society, what does this imply?
6. We are compared to salt in verses 34-35. Salt is used as a preservative and as a flavoring. In relationship to preserving and flavoring, how do I do that in our affluent, materialistic society? What do people really see in my life style? Is Jesus' life style preserved in me? What would a watered-down or compromised type of Christianity look like?

**RESPOND**

Revolution is based upon something that needs to be brought into a new awareness or existence. For the Christian, that is Jesus Christ. The life of Jesus was different from society's in general. His life was—

—opposed to the law when it oppressed people;
—coming to serve, not to be served;

—giving without receiving back;

—total subordination to the point of excluding all loyalties in preference to God;

—not caught up in business, possessions, or personal pleasures of life; He was occupied with God and helping people;

—a contrast to society's life.

In which of the above Christlike characteristics do you need to make commitments to God? How should your life change to become more like Christ's in contrast to society's in general?

*Assignment:*

Read chapter 4 in the text. Think about the questions at the end of the chapter.

Session 4

# The Importance of Listening

*Text:* Chapter 4

*Set Goals for the Session:*

1. Students will recognize the importance of listening.
2. Students will look for opportunities to listen, especially to members of their families.

*Prepare for the Session:*

1. Read chapter 4 in the text.
2. Study carefully the Scripture texts given in this leader's guide.
3. Use as many of the learning activities as possible with your group.
4. Prepare your lesson outline.
5. Prepare a poster showing mechanical listening devices and the human ear.

*Scripture References:*

| | |
|---|---|
| Ephesians 1:13 | Ecclesiastes 5:1-7 |
| Mark 4:1-9 | Daniel 9:17-19 |
| Proverbs 23:22 | Proverbs 15:31-33 |
| Amos 5:21-24 | Proverbs 20:12 |

*Presentation:*

**FOCUS**

1. Divide the class into two equal groups and pair off with a member of each group in each pair. Instruct the members of the first group to tell members of the second group about their most meaningful Christmases. Instruct the second group not to listen to the first group. They should pay no attention—instead, they should look and act distracted. Tell neither group what the other group's instructions are.

   Proceed with the exercise. After the exercise, discuss the following questions:
   - —How did you feel when you wanted to share something and your partner was not listening?
   - —How did you feel when you couldn't listen?
2. Display a poster illustrating mechanical listening devices (telephone, tape recorders, computers, etc.) and another poster showing a human ear.
   - —Have electronic listening devices replaced the human ear? Support your answer.
   - —Is one more personal than the other? Why?
3. Listening is a difficult art. What are some reasons why parents fail to listen to their children? List these on a blackboard or overhead projector.

**DISCOVER**

1. Divide the class into groups of three to five stu-

dents and have them list ways in which the art of listening can be improved. Have each group share their lists with the entire group.

2. Listening is important to recognizing truth. Look at Mark 4:1-9 to see how listening enters into the process of learning new truths. Is there a difference between *listen* in verse 3 and *hear* in verse 9? Have class members share examples from their experiences with their children.
   —When did children "listen" but not "hear"?
   —When have we learned a new truth because we listened to our children?
3. Listening is important for respect. What do Proverbs 23:22 and Ecclesiastes 5:1-7 teach us concerning our respect for God? Are we more apt to listen to God when we have respect for Him? Does it make a difference in our listening to other people if we have respect for them? In what ways?
4. Listening is important for response.

   Amos 5:21-24 Ephesians 1:13
   Daniel 9:17-19 Proverbs 15:31-33

   Our confidence in prayer is determined by our knowledge that God listens to us. How can we know that God listens to our prayers? When we feel that our prayers don't get through to God, is the problem with us or God? Is God always ready and willing to respond to us?

   Salvation is God's gift to us. What part did listening play in our receiving this gift? In what way was our response to this offer dependent on our listening?
5. Discuss the questions at the end of the chapter.

**RESPOND**

1. What will you do this week to open up avenues of listening to each member of your family? What are some hindrances that you will need to deal with?
2. Close with prayer asking God to help you see that the ear is as important as the mouth or eye (Prov. 21:12).

*Assignment:*

1. Spend some time this week listening to other members of your family. Really listen to what they are saying and feeling.
2. Read chapter 5 in the text and think about the questions at the end of the chapter.

Session 5

# Sharing

*Text:* Chapter 5

*Set Goals for the Session:*

1. Students will understand the importance of sharing their lives with other people.
2. Students will know some of the elements of sharing.
3. Students will begin to share their lives with other people.

*Prepare for the Session:*

1. Read chapter 5 of the text.
2. Study carefully the Scripture references in this leader's guide.
3. Prepare your lesson outline.

*Scripture References:*

Proverbs 27:17
Acts 2:42-47
Ephesians 6:2
1 Corinthians 12:1-31
Hebrews 10:23-25

*Presentation:*

**FOCUS**

1. Think of one of the most exciting things that has happened to you. What happened? How many people did you tell? How soon did you tell them?
2. Think of a time when you had to make an important decision. Did you have someone whom you could talk to about the decision? How did you feel about talking to someone or not having anyone to talk to?
3. Think of a time when you experienced a tragedy or had some other burden to bear? Did you talk to someone? What if there had not been anyone else to share this burden?

**DISCOVER**

1. Assign the following Scripture references to individuals or groups:

   Proverbs 27:17 — 1 Corinthians 12:1-31
   Acts 2:42-47 — Hebrews 10:23-25
   Ephesians 6:2

   Ask the following question: What can individuals do together that they cannot do alone? (Sharpen each other's ideas, bear burdens, exhort and stimulate, fellowship, complete each other.)

   What is necessary if this is to happen? (Sharing of our ideas, lives, needs, concerns, joys, sorrows.) To share, we need to remove our masks and reveal ourselves as we really are.
2. Sharing exercises: (Use as many as time allows.)
   a. Divide into groups of two and have each participant briefly tell his favorite Bible story and tell why it is his favorite. The second person

should be able to repeat back what the first person has said to the first person's satisfaction. Then have the second person tell his favorite story and the first person repeat it back.

b. In the total group, encourage each person to share his "dreams" for his life.

c. Ask the following questions:
   1) What was the warmest place in your home when you were six years old?
   2) Who was the warmest person in your life before you were twelve years old?
   3) What is the warmest experience you have had with God at any time in your life?

d. Additional questions:
   1) To me, God is ___.
   2) The best thing about my church is ___.
   3) The hardest thing about my Christian life is ___.
   4) Of all the questions in the world, the one I would like answered most is ___.
   5) I'm afraid (that, of) ___.
   6) I wish ___.
   7) Life in today's world is like ___.

   Allow as many people as possible to answer the above questions, but do not discuss them at length unless there is considerable interest and all group members are entering into the discussion.

These exercises provide an opportunity to share in a nonthreatening manner. They give opportunity for each person to expose himself and his feelings.

3. Discuss the questions for discussion at the end of the chapter.

## RESPOND

1. Think of something which you have wanted to tell some particular person. Decide to tell him or her this week.
2. Close with a prayer asking God to help us to be open and honest with people.

*Assignment:*

1. Carry out your commitment to tell something that is important to someone else this week.
2. Read chapter 6. Think about the questions for discussion at the end of the chapter.

Session 6

# The Role of the Family

*Text:* Chapter 6

*Set Goals for the Session:*

1. Learners will understand the purpose of the family.
2. Learners will evaluate their own family in relationship to the purpose of the family.
3. Learners will plan to provide for the growing independence of their children.

*Prepare for the Session:*

1. Read chapter 6 in the text.
2. Carefully study the Scriptures given in this leader's guide.
3. Prepare a lesson plan.
4. Mimeograph an evaluation form for each student.

*Scripture References:*

Ephesians 6:4
Genesis 18:19
Deuteronomy 6:7
Proverbs 22:6
2 Timothy 3:15
Genesis 2:24

Psalms 78:4

*Presentation:*

**FOCUS**

Parents and children often experience tensions as the children move toward independence and parents want to keep control of the children. Recall and share some of your own childhood experiences and feelings when you wanted to be free of your parents' control.

Recall and share some of your experiences and feelings as parents when your own children want to be free from your control.

**DISCOVER**

1. Have class members look up the following Scriptures to discuss and find answers to the following questions:

   Ephesians 6:4 — Proverbs 22:6
   Genesis 1:18 — 2 Timothy 3:15
   Deuteronomy 6:7 — Genesis 2:24
   Psalm 78:4

   —What are some of the primary responsibilities of parents toward children?
   —How long do parents retain control over their children?
   —How long will the parents' influence last on their children?

2. One of the primary purposes of the family is to rear children to be independent adults. Divide into groups of four to six people to discuss the following questions:

   —What do our children need to know and be in order to survive in an adult world?
   —How can we teach them what they need to know and be?

Report from each group to the total group. James Dobson, in *Hide or Seek* (p. 100), lists some examples of independence in the parental process of letting go of our children. From birth and no responsibility—

—sleeps through the night
—holds own bottle
—sits up, crawls
—learns to walk
—obeys simple instructions
—is toilet trained
—picks up toys and blocks
—helps with household tasks
—feeds dog regularly
—maintains an allowance
—goes to local grocery store
—does homework without being rewarded
—chooses own clothes
—babysits with young child
—has a paper route
—has first date
—gets curfew extended an hour
—has a regular Saturday job
—dates whom he chooses
—has greater freedom with car
—spends money as wishes
—sets own hours to be in
—has few decisions required, great independence
—gets release from home
—gains final release from parental responsibility to young adulthood and full responsibility

Where are your children in this list?

3. Discuss the questions at the end of the chapter.

4. Evaluation:

   Each person should fill out an evaluation form with the following questions:

   1. The ages of my children are ___.
   2. My children's ability to accept responsibility could be described in the following words: ___
   3. When I think of my children being independent from me, I feel ___.
   4. I want my children to accept responsibility in the following areas of life, but they seemingly do not want to do so: ___. Why? ___.
   5. My children want to take responsibility in the following areas of life, but I do not think they are ready to do so: ___. Why? ___.

   Share your evaluation results in the total group.

**RESPOND**

1. On a three-by-five card, make a list of things that your children can do which you are presently doing for them. At home, share with your child that you want to help him/her to become more independent, particularly in the areas listed. You might want to choose one item to work on each week or month.
2. Pray committing your children to God and yourselves to the task of rearing them to be responsible Christian persons.

*Assignment:*

Help your children to do a new thing. Choose one that you have listed on the card.

Read chapter 7 in the text. Think about the questions at the end of the chapter.

Session 7

# The Key Relationship

*Text:* Chapter 7

*Set Goals for the Session:*

1. Students will know that the relationship between the husband and wife is vital to the whole family.
2. Students will learn to equate communication between husband and wife with showing love.
3. Students will determine relationships in their own families which need to be improved.

*Prepare for the Session:*

1. Read chapter 7 in the text.
2. Study carefully the Scripture references in this leader's guide.
3. Prepare your lesson outline.
4. Prepare the instructions for the FOCUS exercise. Put the instructions for each individual on three-by-five cards.

*Scripture References:*

| | |
|---|---|
| Genesis 25:19-34 | Genesis 27:1–28:9 |
| Genesis 26:18-25 | Genesis 37:6-8 |

*Presentation:*

**FOCUS**

Divide the class into groups of three for the FOCUS exercises. Avoid having couples in any of the groups.

1. Discuss the following quotation relating to the treatment of children in a child guidance clinic:

   ". . . When the parents were emotionally close, more invested in each other than either was in the patient, the patient improved. When either parent became more emotionally invested in the patient than in the other parent, the patient immediately and automatically regressed. When the parents were emotionally close, they could do no wrong in their 'management' of the patient. The patient responded well to firmness, permissiveness, punishment, 'taking it out,' or any other management approach. When the parents were 'emotionally divorced,' any and all 'management' approaches were equally unsuccessful" (from *Conjoint Family Therapy*, by Virginia Satir, Science and Behavior Books, Palo Alto, California, 1967, pp. 4-5).

   Do you feel this is a reliable statement: How do parents keep emotionally close?

2. In your groups of three, do the following:
   Pass out envelope number 1 to each group. They are to follow the instructions, but not talk about them. After they complete the first exercise, pass out envelope 2 to each group. Let them do this exercise, and then pass out envelope 3 and complete the exercise.

*Contents of envelope 1:* Three cards of instructions

Person 1: (read this to your group) The first person in your group is to share his current goals for his family. He is to take one minute and another person in the group will time him.

Person 2: (not to be read to the group) Do not interrupt person 1 while talking. When he is finished say, "That was very interesting," and make no further comments.

Person 3: Same instructions as for person 2.

*Contents of envelope 2:* Three cards of instructions

Person 1: (not to be read to the group) Do not interrupt person 2 while speaking. When he is finished, say, "That was very interesting. I was interested in what you said about ___."

Person 2: (read this to your group) In one minute, share your current goals for your family.

Person 3: Same instructions as person 1.

*Contents of envelope 3:* Three cards of instructions

Person 1: (not to be read to the group) Do not interrupt person 3 while speaking. When he is finished say, "I was quite interested in ___." Make other comments on what he shared, even asking questions. Person 2 will be joining you in this.

Person 2: Listen to person 3 without interrupting him. Join in with person 1, questioning and making statements about what was said. Indicate how what person 3 said may have benefited you.

Person 3: In one minute share your goals for your family.

Discuss in your groups how each person felt as the people responded to what was said.

Bring the groups back together as a class and summarize the feelings discovered in the exercise. (They didn't listen to me. I'm not important. They listened. I'm important, loved, etc.)

Allow time for additional discussion of this exercise according to interest.

**DISCOVER**

1. In groups of three to five persons, read the following Scripture references and discuss the questions:

   Genesis 25:19-34 Genesis 27:1–28-9
   Genesis 26:18-25 Genesis 37:6-9

   a. What was Isaac's reason for loving Esau?
   b. What was Rebekah's reason for loving Jacob?
   c. How did Isaac and Rebekah have a relationship which was broken down? (Compare with the destructive ways of handling communications on page 46 of the text.)
   d. What were the results in this breakdown?

   Allow time for each small group to share their findings with the total group and discuss as time and interests allow.

2. Question: What are the goals in parenting? (To rear a child to be independent of his parents.) Do you agree or disagree with the author's state-

ment: "Emancipation is the process in the family that sets the child free. A good relationship between husband and wife greatly aids this process" (p. 46): What does this say about the role of the father in parenting?

3. List as many ways as you can think of to communicate love.
4. Discuss the questions at the end of the chapter.

**RESPOND**

What do you see in your relationship with your spouse that needs to be improved? What will you do this week to improve this relationship?

*Assignment:*

1. Look for new ways to communicate your love to your spouse this week.
2. Read chapter 8 in the text.

Session 8

# Providing a Place

*Text:* Chapter 8

*Set Goals for the Session:*

1. Students will know the importance of providing a place for family members to feel that they belong and are accepted.
2. Students will learn how to provide a place for family members to belong.
3. Students will plan to begin providing a place where family members can belong.

*Prepare for the Session:*

1. Read chapter 8 in the text.
2. Study the Scripture references in the leader's guide.
3. Prepare a lesson plan.
4. Invite members to sit on the panel discussion.

Prepare a list of discussion questions for them to have for their own preparation.

5. You may want to ask people ahead of time to participate in the role play.
6. Provide three-by-five cards for RESPOND.

*Scripture References:*

Ephesians 5:21–6:4

*Presentation:*

**FOCUS**

Have each person draw two charts. The first chart will reflect his childhood home as he remembers it. The second will reflect his present family.

1. Draw a chart of your childhood family as you remember it. Use circles to represent each family member. Draw circles of different sizes to represent the power of each family member with the largest circle representing the person who had the most power. Draw the circles close together or far apart to represent closeness of family members to each other.
2. Using the same instructions as in 1, draw a chart of your present family.
3. Ask individuals to volunteer to share their charts.
4. Answer the following questions:
   a. How do you feel about your childhood home experiences as reflected in the chart?
   b. How do you feel about your present family experiences as reflected in the chart?
   c. Would you consider these "open" or "closed" families?

**DISCOVER**

1. In groups of five to seven people, study Ephesians 5:21–6:4. The following questions might guide your thinking:

a. What are some characteristics of "open" homes and families?
b. What are some characteristics of "closed" homes and families?
c. Give specific examples of what happens in "open" and "closed" families.

Allow adequate time for discussion and then have each group report to the entire class.

2. Panel discussion: You might want to have a panel discussion for part of the class period. People who could participate might be a parent, a teenager, a pastor, a teacher, a youth counselor, or others who work with young people or families. You could use the questions in exercise 1. Also take time to talk about what parents can do to keep the home and family an "open" place. Allow time for the class to ask questions and make comments.
3. Discuss as a total group:
What are some things that cause conflict between parents and children in your home? Are these really important issues? How are the conflicts resolved? How do the people involved in the conflicts feel after the conflicts are resolved?
4. Discuss the questions at the end of the chapter.

**RESPOND**

Have each person respond individually to the following:

"I think of the color ___ when I think of my present home relationships." Why?

What do I need to do to make my home a more "open" place where family members feel they belong? What will I do this week about this? Write your answer on a three-by-five card.

*Assignment:*

1. Look for opportunities this week to make your home a more "open" and accepting place.
2. Read chapter 9 in the text. Think about the questions at the end of the chapter.

Session 9

# Providing Limits

*Text:* Chapter 9

*Set Goals for the Session:*

1. Students will know the importance of discipline for their children.
2. Students will find some principles of discipline.
3. Students will evaluate their own disciplinary procedures.

*Prepare for the Session:*

1. Read chapter 9 in the text.
2. Study the Scripture references given in the leader's guide.
3. Prepare a lesson outline.
4. Prepare AGREE and DISAGREE signs for the opening exercise.

*Scripture References:*

1 Samuel 3:11-14
Proverbs 13:24
Proverbs 22:6
Ephesians 6:4

*Presentation:*

**FOCUS**

1. Agree/Disagree. Make the following statement: "Permissiveness can bring confidence and the capacity to children to express their feelings and thoughts." Ask your students if they agree or disagree. If possible, have all those who agree stand on one side of the room under the AGREE sign and all those who disagree stand on the other side under the DISAGREE sign. Give opportunity for members of each side to persuade the other side to join them. Have them explain their reasons for their response to the statement.

2. Neighbor nudging: Pair off. Ask each pair to share together about childhood experiences when their parents disciplined them. What did they do to deserve discipline? How were they disciplined? How did they feel about it?
   Then share some of your experiences as a parent disciplining your children. What did they do to deserve discipline? How did you discipline them? How did they feel about it. How did you feel about it?
   After a few minutes of sharing, give opportunity for some pairs to share their experiences and feelings with the total group.

**DISCOVER**

1. Scripture search
   Divide the class into groups of five or six people. Have each group study the following Scriptures:

   1 Samuel 3:11-14 Proverbs 22:6
   Proverbs 13:24 Ephesians 6:4

   The group should feel free to add other Scripture

references. Write a list of as many things as you can think of about discipline from your study. List both principles and applications.

Each group should later share their lists with the entire class.

2. Share with your class the discussion on page 57 of three behavior zones: green zone—acceptable behavior; yellow zone—tolerable behavior; red zone—unacceptable behavior. In three columns on the chalkboard or overhead projector, have the class list kinds of behavior that fall into the three zones. Be as specific as possible.
   —Do all class members agree on what belongs in each zone?
   —Will a certain kind of behavior always fall into the same zone?
3. Make a list of rules for discipline.
   —When do you discipline?
   —For what do you discipline?
   —How do you discipline?
   —Who disciplines?

   Do class members have any rules for discipline in their homes?
4. Talk about the questions for discussion at the end of the chapter.

**RESPOND**

1. Have each member decide what he needs to change in his discipline procedures.
2. Pray asking God's guidance in helping children to come to independent maturity.

Session 10

# The Birthright

*Text:* Chapter 10

*Set Goals for the Session:*

1. Students will know the importance of affirming their children.
2. Students will learn how to affirm their children.
3. Students will make plans for affirmation of their children.

*Prepare for the Session:*

1. Read chapter 10 in the text.
2. Study the Scripture references given in the leader's guide.
3. Prepare a lesson plan.
4. Have paper and pencils ready for the RESPOND exercise.

*Scripture References:*

Exodus 13:2, 12-16
Genesis 25:27-34
Deuteronomy 21:15-17
1 Chronicles 5:1-2

*Presentation:*

**FOCUS**

Give opportunity for your adults to share childhood memories of times when their parents or other family members made them feel as if "I'm special." Allow a short time for class members to recall these times and then have several people share their experiences.

**DISCOVER**

1. In the Old Testament, the birthright was a very important way of telling the oldest son that he was special. He was given privileges beyond his brothers. Among the Israelites, God had special claim upon the firstborn, at least from the time of the Exodus.

   Divide the class into groups of four to six people and have them study the following Scriptures to discover all that they can about the birthright.

   Exodus 13:2,12-16 Deuteronomy 21:15-17
   Genesis 25:27-34 1 Chronicles 5:1-2

   Have each group list everything they can discover about the birthright. Then give opportunity for each group to report to the total group.
2. Showing favoritism is one way that parents do not pass an "I'm special" birthright on to their children.
   —How might parents show favoritism to one child over another?
   —Why might parents show favoritism to one child?
   —What happens to children, both the one being favored and the one being mistreated, when parents show favoritism?
3. List as many ways as you can think of to tell a

child "You're special." What happens to a child when he knows he is special?

4. Discuss the questions at the end of the chapter.

**RESPOND**

1. Write a letter to your child (or each child) telling them why he is special. Give it to him at the next meal.
2. What will you do this week to tell your child that he is special?

*Assignment:*

1. In as many ways as possible, tell your child "You're special" this week.
2. Read chapter 11 in the text.

Session 11

# Looking at a Process

*Text:* Chapter 11

*Set Goals for the Session:*

1. Students will recognize that their children are created to be different from everyone else.
2. Students will recognize that their children have a right to be free to discover for themselves where they fit into God's plan.

*Prepare for the Session:*

1. Read chapter 11 in the text.
2. Study the Scripture references in the leader's guide.
3. Prepare a lesson plan.

*Scripture References:*

| | |
|---|---|
| Hebrews 11 | 1 Peter 3:9 |
| Genesis 4:1-5 | Ezekiel 18:20 |
| Romans 14:12 | Genesis 25:23-28 |

*Presentation:*

**FOCUS**

1. Have each student list on paper some of the ways his children differ from one another. You might suggest some of the following traits to consider: eating habits, study habits, neatness, friendliness toward others, taste for music, sports interest, ways they display affection, favorite subjects, love for church, goals in life.
   After time has been allowed for writing these comparisons, have each student read his list to the group.
2. After the comparison of child with child has been made, have the students list in the same manner ways in which they themselves differ from their children.

**DISCOVER**

1. The Value of a Person: Discuss the following questions:
   —How did God value the worth of many characters in the Old Testament? See Hebrews 11. What has God done with the sins of people mentioned in Hebrews 11?
   —Have someone read 2 Peter 3:9. Discuss the question: How much is a person worth to God?
   —How do we measure the value of our children? By the satisfaction we get from them? By good manners or good looks? Intelligence? Other ways? What happens to children when their value is measured in these ways?
   —How should we measure the value of children?

2. All People Are Not Alike: Discuss the following questions:
   —What do we learn about siblings from Genesis 4:1-5? Are parents to blame if one child seems to be less spiritual than his brother or sister, or if one grows up to be a Christian and the other a non-Christian? For biblical help in answering the above questions, have someone read Ezekiel 18:20 and Romans 14:12.
   —What do we learn from Genesis 25:23-28? Are Isaac and Rebekah to be commended for the ways in which each accepted the differences between their sons? Why?
   —When Christian parents perceive that one of their children pleases them more than another, how should they deal with the problem? Is it the child's problem or their own?
3. The Freedom of a Person: Discuss the following questions:
   —Ask the students how they think they would feel if their eighteen- or nineteen-year-old child came to them with the announcement that he is going to be a missionary in a foreign land.
   —How can we parents help our children discover where they fit into God's plan for them?
4. Talk about the questions at the end of the chapter.

**RESPOND**

It is imperative that our children discover who they are as individuals and where they fit, with all their uniqueness and gifts, into God's universal plan. Are you, as a parent, prepared to accept God's plan for your child, even if it conflicts with your own plan for him?

Close with prayer, asking God to help you guide your children into His plan for them.

*Assignment:*

1. Read chapter 12 in the text.
2. Look for the unique characteristics in your children this week.

Session 12

# They Are OK

*Text:* Chapter 12

*Set Goals for the Session:*

1. Students will know that they can feel good about themselves.
2. Students will know some ways to make people, especially their children, feel good about themselves.
3. Students will plan to help themselves and their children feel good about themselves.

*Prepare for the Session:*

1. Read chapter 12 in the text.
2. Study the Scripture references in the leader's guide.
3. Prepare a lesson plan.

*Scripture References:*

Genesis 1:24-31 2 Corinthians 5:17

Psalm 8:1-9
Matthew 22:37-39
Romans 8:1-39
Galatians 4:1-7
Ephesians 2:1-7
1 Peter 2:9-10

*Presentation:*

**FOCUS**

Neighbor nudging: In pairs, ask your learners to share experiences from their lives, either as children or adults, that made them feel "I'm OK." After allowing two or three minutes for sharing, ask the learners to share experiences from their lives that made them feel, "I'm not OK."

**DISCOVER**

1. Scripture search

   Invite your group to share Scriptures which tell them, "You're OK." Encourage the students to think of the Scriptures themselves and read them. Some that might be mentioned are Genesis 1:24-31, Psalm 8:1-9, Matthew 22:37-39, Romans 8:1-39, 2 Corinthians 5:17, Galatians 4:1-7, Ephesians 2:1-7, 1 Peter 2:9-10. Add others that you or the students will think of.

   This exercise is designed to show that God feels good about us and that He wants us to feel good about ourselves. We can accept ourselves as we are in God's grace and experience His forgiveness and acceptance.

2. Dr. Wagemaker makes a reference to Thomas Harris's book, *I'm OK, You're OK*, and points out what he feels are three basic parts of each person—child, parent, adult.

   —What are some basic characteristics of each part?

   —Share experiences that show when you responded with characteristics of each part.

—How can a person move from responding according to the "child" or "parent" in him to responding as an "adult"?

3. "I'm OK, You're OK"
   There are four basic positions people have in relationship to each other:
   "I'm not OK, You're OK."
   "I'm not OK, You're not OK."
   "I'm OK, You're not OK."
   "I'm OK, You're OK."
   —How do these positions develop?
   —How do we come to the position of saying, "I'm OK"?
4. Conflict resolution between parents and children provides an opportunity for building self-respect. Role-play your response to the following situation:
   Your daughter has returned home from a date more than an hour past the agreed time. This has happened several times in the past month.
   —How do you respond? Is your response characteristic of the "child," "parent," or "adult" in you?
   —How does your response make you feel?
   —How does your response make your daughter feel?
   —Is there a better response?
   —How will you finally resolve this conflict?
5. Answer the questions at the end of the chapter.

**RESPOND**

1. Write a prayer to God thanking Him for your "OK" position because of His forgiveness and grace. Also, ask Him to help you make those around you feel "OK."
2. What do you need to do this week to make other

people around you, especially your family members, feel "OK"?

*Assignment:*

1. Look for opportunities to make other people feel good about themselves.
2. Read chapter 13 in the text.

Session 13

# The Solution, a Starting Point

*Text:* Chapter 13

*Set Goals for the Session:*

1. Students will know the importance of allowing people to be themselves and have their own opinions.
2. Students will know some ways to resolve conflicts between parents and children.
3. Students will respond to their personal needs in conflict resolution.

*Prepare for the Session:*

1. Read chapter 13 in the text.
2. Study carefully the Scripture reference in the leader's guide.
3. Prepare a lesson plan and any lecture input you will give.

*Scripture Reference:*
Romans 14:1-23

*Presentation:*

**FOCUS**

In groups of four to six people, discuss the following questions:

—Why do parents and children have conflicts?
—Do you feel that these conflicts are mostly your fault or your children's fault?
—What can you do to resolve these conflicts?

Report to the total group.

**DISCOVER**

1. Again, in your small groups of four to six people, study Romans 14:1-23. List as many principles and ideas as you can find for getting along with others. Allow adequate time for discussion, then have each group report to the total group.

2. Conflict Resolution
Thomas Gordon, in *Parent Effectiveness Training*, gives some ideas on child rearing and conflict resolution. These ideas are also picked up and expanded by Earl Gaulke in *You Can Have A Family Where Everybody Wins*. Gaulke's book is a Christian perspective on parent effectiveness training. Check your church and public libraries for these books. While we must be careful in accepting all the underlying assumptions of parent effectiveness training, it does offer many helpful ideas.
Parents must accept the person of their child. They do not need to accept his behavior. There are some areas of behavior acceptable to the parents but which create a problem for the child

because he is thwarted in satisfying his need. Other actions present no problem. Still other behavior creates a problem for the parents because the child is interfering with the parent's satisfying a need of his own (see diagram below).

| Areas of acceptance | Child owns the problem | Child's behavior is a problem to parent |
|---|---|---|
| | No problem | |
| Areas of non-acceptance | Parent owns the problem | Child's behavior is a problem to him. |

Review the conflicts discussed at the beginning of the session. Are these behaviors in the realm of acceptance or nonacceptance? Who owns the problem in the behavior?
It is important to recognize who owns the problem because that will determine how we respond to the problem (see diagram below).

| Acceptable behavior | Child owns problem (Active listening) | We own the problem: Conflict of needs (Method III) |
|---|---|---|
| | No problem (Reinforce) | |
| Unacceptable behavior | I own the problem (Confront—"I message") | We own the problem: Conflict of values (Model, consult, pray) |

Active listening involves listening for the feeling behind the verbal communication. It communicates acceptance both verbally and nonverbally. Think back to the conflicts previously discussed.

What are your children really trying to tell you?

What are you really trying to tell your children?

"I messages" simply tell the child how some unacceptable behavior is making the parent feel. They are generally constructed as follows: "When you ___ I feel ___ because ___."

Construct an "I message" in response to a conflict with your children.

Method III involves finding a solution to a conflict which is agreeable to both parent and child. (Method I—parents resort to power so the solution is unacceptable to the child. Method II—parents give in so the solution is unacceptable to them.)

Find solutions to your previously discussed conflicts which will be acceptable to both you and your children.

3. Talk about the questions at the end of the chapter.

**RESPOND**

1. Determine one conflict that you will try to resolve this week. What will you do about it?
2. Pray.

# Suggested Reading


Briscoe, D. Stuart, *Where Was the Church When the Youth Exploded?* (Zondervan)

Gaulke, Earl H., *You Can Have a Family Where Everybody Wins* (Concordia)

Ginott, Haim, G., *Between Parent and Teenager* (MacMillan)

Ginott, Haim, G., *Between Parent and Child* (MacMillan)

Gordon, Thomas, *Parent Effectiveness Training* (P. H. Wyden)

Granberg, Lars I., *For Adults Only* (Zondervan)

Harris, Thomas, *I'm OK, You're OK* (Harper and Row)

Larson, Bruce, *Marriage Is for Living* (Zondervan)

Mayers, Marvin K., and Koechel, David D., *Love Goes on Forever* (Zondervan)

Mow, Anna B., *Your Child* (Zondervan)

Mow, Anna B., *Your Teen-ager and You* (Zondervan)

Narramore, Bruce, *Help! I'm a Parent* (Zondervan)

Narramore, Bruce, *A Guide to Child Rearing* (Zondervan)

Osborne, Cecil, *The Art of Understanding Your Mate* (Zondervan)

Osborne, Cecil, *The Art of Understanding Yourself* (Zondervan)

Wiese, Bennard R., and Steinmetz, Urban G., *Everything You Need to Know to Stay Married and Like It!* (Zondervan)

Wilkerson, David, and Wilkerson, Don, *Counseling the Untapped Generation* (Zondervan)